THIRD EDITION

Skills for Success
LISTENING AND SPEAKING

Robert Freire | Tamara Jones

198 Madison Avenue
New York, NY 10016 USA

Great Clarendon Street, Oxford, OX2 6DP, United Kingdom

Oxford University Press is a department of the University of Oxford. It furthers the University's objective of excellence in research, scholarship, and education by publishing worldwide. Oxford is a registered trade mark of Oxford University Press in the UK and in certain other countries

© Oxford University Press 2020

The moral rights of the author have been asserted

First published in 2020

2024 2023 2022
10 9 8 7 6 5 4

No unauthorized photocopying

All rights reserved. No part of this publication may be reproduced, stored in a retrieval system, or transmitted, in any form or by any means, without the prior permission in writing of Oxford University Press, or as expressly permitted by law, by licence or under terms agreed with the appropriate reprographics rights organization. Enquiries concerning reproduction outside the scope of the above should be sent to the ELT Rights Department, Oxford University Press, at the address above

You must not circulate this work in any other form and you must impose this same condition on any acquirer

Links to third party websites are provided by Oxford in good faith and for information only. Oxford disclaims any responsibility for the materials contained in any third party website referenced in this work

ISBN: 978 0 19 490498 8 STUDENT BOOK 4B WITH IQ ONLINE PACK
ISBN: 978 0 19 490486 5 STUDENT BOOK 4B AS PACK COMPONENT
ISBN: 978 0 19 490540 4 IQ ONLINE STUDENT WEBSITE

Printed in China

This book is printed on paper from certified and well-managed sources

ACKNOWLEDGEMENTS

Back cover photograph: Oxford University Press building/David Fisher

The author and publisher are grateful to those who have given permission to reproduce the following extracts and adaptations of copyright material:
p. 5 from "Leadership isn't just for the boss" by CBC Radio-Canada, 31 July 2017. © CBC Radio-Canada. Reproduced by permission; p. 11 Hammett, Pete. "3 Ways to Break Out of Your Executive Bubble." Audio blog post. Leading Effectively. Center for Creative Leadership, 2007. www.ccl.org. Drawn from *Unbalanced Influence: Recognizing and Resolving the Impact of Myth and Paradox in Executive Performance*, Davies-Black Publishing, Copyright © 2007 Pete Hammett. Reproduced by permission; p. 35 from "Colour Schemes: How Colours Make You Buy" from Under the Influence with Terry O'Reilly, 10 May 2018, CBC Radio. © Terry O'Reilly. Reproduced by permission; p. 62 from "A lament for the sad state of financial literacy among young people" by CBC Radio-Canada, The Sunday Edition, 6 March 2016. © CBC Radio-Canada. Reproduced by permission; p. 154 adapted from "The Power of Serendipity" from CBS News Sunday Morning, 7 October 2007. © CBS News. Reproduced by permission of CBS News Archives; p. 180 from "Automation and Us" by CBC Radio-Canada, 5 October 2014, 6 March 2016. © CBC Radio-Canada. Reproduced by permission.

Illustrations by: pp. 81, 82, 96, 99 Mark Duffin; p. 73 Joe Taylor.

We would also like to thank the following for permission to reproduce the following photographs: **123rf:** pp. 5 (informal business meeting/Mark Bowden), 36 (BP logo/Alexandr Blinov), 57 (student/Antonio Diaz), 70 (parents holding infant/Mark Bowden), 83 (kerosene lamp/Oleksandr Kozak), 104 (Peking duck/Mikhail Valeev), 105 (drone/Goce Risteski), 119 (chocolate ice cream/Hans Geel), 155 (coffee beans/Ilja Generalov), 156 (GPS/Igor Stevanovic), 173 (popsicles/Jennifer Barrow); **Alamy:** pp. 2 (conductor and orchestra/imageBROKER), 11 (business meeting/MBI), 15 (colleagues working together/Albert Shakirov), 16 (John Donahoe/ZUMA Press, Inc.), 18 (student listening to podcast/Dan Grytsku), 22 (supervisor giving talk to employees/Hero Images Inc.), 30 (Agatha Christie/Everett Collection Historical), 32 (boy in messy room/Big Cheese Photo LLC), 38 (Owens Corning advertisement/Cal Sport Media), 49 (stressed woman/Andriy Popov), 52 (woman voting/Hero Images Inc.), 54 (Seijin no Hi celebration/dpa picture alliance), 62 (woman counting money/Hero Images Inc.), 78 (space rocket/Konstantin Shaklein), 104 (shark liver oil/BSIP SA), 108 (man assembling drone/Montgomery Martin), 109 (organic sign/David Angel), 113 (family walking/Carmen K. Sisson/Cloudybright), 135 (intern and supervisor/LightField Studios Inc.), 147 (women leaving college library/Adam Bronkhorst), 152 (abseiling in cave/Cavan), 154 (doctor examining x-ray/Blend Images), 156 (pacemaker/Phanie), (Velcro/Stocksnapper), 158 (magnetron/Aleksandr Volkov), 166 (brain injury/BSIP SA), (Phineas Gage/ART Collection), (skull graphic/BSIP SA), 168 (nomad with camel/Guillem Lopez), 170 (professor lecturing/Reeldeal Images), 172 (raised hands/Wavebreak Media ltd), 176 (man photographing nature/Cultura Creative RF), 177 (woman in deep sea submersible/SeaTops), 182 (doctor and patient/Hero Images Inc.), 190 (traffic/Don Bartell), 201 (man with personal assistant/Image navi - QxQ images), 203 (family on video call/Tetra Images, LLC); **Getty:** pp. cover (prismatic background of binary code/KTSDESIGN/SCIENCE PHOTO LIBRARY), 4 (woman with award/Hill Street Studios), 6 (restaurant manager and employee/andresr), 8 (boss and employee in shop/andresr), 13 (suggestion box/Randy Faris), 20 (female speaker/Caiaimage/Martin Barraud), 25 (sports team coach/SolStock), 26 (modern workplace/Bloomberg), 45 (employee leaving work/Hero Images), 51 (woman looking at notes/PeopleImages), 54 (Quinceañera/Pixelchrome Inc), 55 (women in laundromat/Hero Images), 72 (graduates/Â© Hiya Images/Corbis), 77 (man moving house/Matthias Ritzmann), 87 (circuit board/TimeStopper), 88 (Gordon Moore/Justin Sullivan), 89 (tech items/Yuri_Arcurs), 94 (solar windows/Ashley Cooper), 101 (engineers working on turbines/Westend61), 102 (man spraying crops/D-Keine), 107 (farmer with tablet/Ariel Skelley), 117 (scientists monitoring bananas/chinaface), 123 (fat chicken/Suphanat Wongsanuphat), 125 (underwater grown tomatoes/Alexis Rosenfeld), 126 (winter climbers /David Trood), 129 (colleagues chatting in office/Ezra Bailey), 130 (Scott Nash/The Washington Post), (John Paul DeJoria/John M. Heller), (Michael Acton Smith/Oli Scarff/Staff), 132 (woman looking at whiteboard/andresr), 134 (man and woman reviewing CVs/Hero Images), 136 (woman delivering drinks/Paul Bradbury), 137 (woman in office/electravk), 139 (interns at tech company/Anchiy), 141 (women shaking hands/laflor), 143 (friends in café/ferrantraite), 145 (hand petting rhino/Suneet Bhardwaj), (woman walking down steps/gradyreese), 151 (committee job interview/filadendron), 162 (twin babies/YinYang), 178 (miniature drone/Andre Dancer/EyeEm), 193 (car engineer/Monty Rakusen), 201 (woman hugging robot/NurPhoto), (medical care robot/JIJI PRESS/Stringer); **OUP:** p. 35 (smiling woman); **Shutterstock:** pp. 14 (employee at door/Dean Drobot), 28 (tidy work desk/thodonal88), 35 (colorful ties/Fedor Selivanov), 36 (McDonalds sign/Jonathan Weiss), (Tiffany box/AlesiaKan), (Easyjet airplane/NUI BLANCO), (NYC taxi/elbud), (Apple logo/r.classen), (Starbucks logo/CHALERMPHON SRISANG), (Louboutin shoes/andersphoto), 37 (pink insulation in house/Rachid Jalayanadeja), 40 (waterfront promenade/Malgorzata Litkowska), 41 (messy work desk/Andrey_Popov), 46 (casually dressed man/Rido), (formal dressed man/Bangkok Click Studio), 57 (teacher/Monkey Business Images), 60 (man thinking/Syda Productions), 64 (friends laughing/Monkey Business Images), 66 (laptop/LightField Studios), 84 (waterwheel/nikolansfoto), 110 (large plate of fries/stockcreations), 112 (chocolates/Iakov Filimonov), 114 (ice cream sundae/stockcreations), 119 (strawberry ice cream/beats1), 122 (men in café/Sjale), 123 (ripe raspberries/Olexandr Panchenko), (moldy raspberries/Andrzej Rostek), (slim chicken/Jakkrit Phomwong), 156 (cookies/Mouse family), (rechargeable batteries/art_photo_sib), (tea/Arancio), 159 (lightbulb moment/Billion Photos), 161 (prehistoric cave paintings/thipjang), 174 (Rosetta Stone/Claudio Divizia), 180 (factory with robots/AlexLMX), (self-checkout/frantic00), (robot vacuum cleaner/Jtal), (robot arm/THINK A), 183 (pilots in cockpit/Skycolors), 184 (automation concept/PopTika), 187 (adult photographing scenery/ProStockStudio), 188 (driverless car/Snapic_PhotoProduction), 191 (smart home/zhu difeng), 193 (dentist and patient/Africa Studio), (dietician/Stasique), 194 (self-driving truck/Tony Avelar/AP), 195 (3D printer/science photo), 198 (robot typing on computer/Andrey_Popov), 200 (woman talking on phone/Antonio Guillem); **Third party:** pp. 30 (Leon Heppel/Office of NIH History and Stetten Museum, U.S. National Institutes of Health), 57 (Rachel Weinstein/Rachel Weinstein/Adulting school), 80 (Hannah Herbst/Julie Herbst).

ACKNOWLEDGMENTS

We would like to acknowledge the teachers from all over the world who participated in the development process and review of *Q: Skills for Success* Third Edition.

USA

Kate Austin, Avila University, MO; **Sydney Bassett**, Auburn Global University, AL; **Michael Beamer**, USC, CA; **Renae Betten**, CBU, CA; **Pepper Boyer**, Auburn Global University, AL; **Marina Broeder**, Mission College, CA; **Thomas Brynmore**, Auburn Global University, AL; **Britta Burton**, Mission College, CA; **Kathleen Castello**, Mission College, CA; **Teresa Cheung**, North Shore Community College, MA; **Shantall Colebrooke**, Auburn Global University, AL; **Kyle Cooper**, Troy University, AL; **Elizabeth Cox**, Auburn Global University, AL; **Ashley Ekers**, Auburn Global University, AL; **Rhonda Farley**, Los Rios Community College, CA; **Marcus Frame**, Troy University, AL; **Lora Glaser**, Mission College, CA; **Hala Hamka**, Henry Ford College, MI; **Shelley A. Harrington**, Henry Ford College, MI; **Barrett J. Heusch**, Troy University, AL; **Beth Hill**, St. Charles Community College, MO; **Patty Jones**, Troy University, AL; **Tom Justice**, North Shore Community College, MA; **Robert Klein**, Troy University, AL; **Patrick Maestas**, Auburn Global University, AL; **Elizabeth Merchant**, Auburn Global University, AL; **Rosemary Miketa**, Henry Ford College, MI; **Myo Myint**, Mission College, CA; **Lance Noe**, Troy University, AL; **Irene Pannatier**, Auburn Global University, AL; **Annie Percy**, Troy University, AL; **Erin Robinson**, Troy University, AL; **Juliane Rosner**, Mission College, CA; **Mary Stevens**, North Shore Community College, MA; **Pamela Stewart**, Henry Ford College, MI; **Karen Tucker**, Georgia Tech, GA; **Loreley Wheeler**, North Shore Community College, MA; **Amanda Wilcox**, Auburn Global University, AL; **Heike Williams**, Auburn Global University, AL

Canada

Angelika Brunel, Collège Ahuntsic, QC; **David Butler**, English Language Institute, BC; **Paul Edwards**, Kwantlen Polytechnic University, BC; **Cody Hawver**, University of British Columbia, BC; **Olivera Jovovic**, Kwantlen Polytechnic University, BC; **Tami Moffatt**, University of British Columbia, BC; **Dana Pynn**, Vancouver Island University, BC

Latin America

Georgette Barreda, SENATI, Peru; **Claudia Cecilia Díaz Romero**, Colegio América, Mexico; **Jeferson Ferro**, Uninter, Brazil; **Mayda Hernández**, English Center, Mexico; **Jose Ixtaccihusatl**, Instituto Tecnológico de Tecomatlán, Mexico; **Andreas Paulus Pabst**, CBA Idiomas, Brazil; **Amanda Carla Pas**, Instituição de Ensino Santa Izildinha, Brazil; **Allen Quesada Pacheco**, University of Costa Rica, Costa Rica; **Rolando Sánchez**, Escuela Normal de Tecámac, Mexico; **Luis Vasquez**, CESNO, Mexico

Asia

Asami Atsuko, Jissen Women's University, Japan; **Rene Bouchard**, Chinzei Keiai Gakuen, Japan; **Francis Brannen**, Sangmyung University, South Korea; **Haeyun Cho**, Sogang University, South Korea; **Daniel Craig**, Sangmyung University, South Korea; **Thomas Cuming**, Royal Melbourne Institute of Technology, Vietnam; **Nguyen Duc Dat**, OISP, Vietnam; **Wayne Devitte**, Tokai University, Japan; **James D. Dunn**, Tokai University, Japan; **Fergus Hann**, Tokai University, Japan; **Michael Hood**, Nihon University College of Commerce, Japan; **Hideyuki Kashimoto**, Shijonawate High School, Japan; **David Kennedy**, Nihon University, Japan; **Anna Youngna Kim**, Sogang University, South Korea; **Jae Phil Kim**, Sogang University, South Korea; **Jaganathan Krishnasamy**, GB Academy, Malaysia; **Peter Laver**, Incheon National University, South Korea; **Hung Hoang Le**, Ho Chi Minh City University of Technology, Vietnam; **Hyon Sook Lee**, Sogang University, South Korea; **Ji-seon Lee**, Iruda English Institute, South Korea; **Joo Young Lee**, Sogang University, South Korea; **Phung Tu Luc**, Ho Chi Minh City University of Technology, Vietnam; **Richard Mansbridge**, Hoa Sen University, Vietnam; **Kahoko Matsumoto**, Tokai University, Japan; **Elizabeth May**, Sangmyung University, South Korea; **Naoyuki Naganuma**, Tokai University, Japan; **Hiroko Nishikage**, Taisho University, Japan; **Yongjun Park**, Sangji University, South Korea; **Paul Rogers**, Dongguk University, South Korea; **Scott Schafer**, Inha University, South Korea; **Michael Schvaudner**, Tokai University, Japan; **Brendan Smith**, RMIT University, School of Languages and English, Vietnam; **Peter Snashall**, Huachiew Chalermprakiet University, Thailand; **Makoto Takeda**, Sendai Third Senior High School, Japan; **Peter Talley**, Mahidol University, Faculty of ICT, Thailand; **Byron Thigpen**, Sogang University, South Korea; **Junko Yamaai**, Tokai University, Japan; **Junji Yamada**, Taisho University, Japan; **Sayoko Yamashita**, Jissen Women's University, Japan; **Masami Yukimori**, Taisho University, Japan

Middle East and North Africa

Sajjad Ahmad, Taibah University, Saudi Arabia; **Basma Alansari**, Taibah University, Saudi Arabia; **Marwa Al-ashqar**, Taibah University, Saudi Arabia; **Dr. Rashid Al-Khawaldeh**, Taibah University, Saudi Arabia; **Mohamed Almohamed**, Taibah University, Saudi Arabia; **Dr Musaad Alrahaili**, Taibah University, Saudi Arabia; **Hala Al Sammar**, Kuwait University, Kuwait; **Ahmed Alshammari**, Taibah University, Saudi Arabia; **Ahmed Alshamy**, Taibah University, Saudi Arabia; **Doniazad sultan AlShraideh**, Taibah University, Saudi Arabia; **Sahar Amer**, Taibah University, Saudi Arabia; **Nabeela Azam**, Taibah University, Saudi Arabia; **Hassan Bashir**, Edex, Saudi Arabia; **Rachel Batchilder**, College of the North Atlantic, Qatar; **Nicole Cuddie**, Community College of Qatar, Qatar; **Mahdi Duris**, King Saud University, Saudi Arabia; **Ahmed Ege**, Institute of Public Administration, Saudi Arabia; **Magda Fadle**, Victoria College, Egypt; **Mohammed Hassan**, Taibah University, Saudi Arabia; **Tom Hodgson**, Community College of Qatar, Qatar; **Ayub Agbar Khan**, Taibah University, Saudi Arabia; **Cynthia Le Joncour**, Taibah University, Saudi Arabia; **Ruari Alexander MacLeod**, Community College of Qatar, Qatar; **Nasir Mahmood**, Taibah University, Saudi Arabia; **Duria Salih Mahmoud**, Taibah University, Saudi Arabia; **Ameera McKoy**, Taibah University, Saudi Arabia; **Chaker Mhamdi**, Buraimi University College, Oman; **Baraa Shiekh Mohamed**, Community College of Qatar, Qatar; **Abduleelah Mohammed**, Taibah University, Saudi Arabia; **Shumaila Nasir**, Taibah University, Saudi Arabia; **Kevin Onwordi**, Taibah University, Saudi Arabia; **Dr. Navid Rahmani**, Community College of Qatar, Qatar; **Dr. Sabah Salman Sabbah**, Community College of Qatar, Qatar; **Salih**, Taibah University, Saudi Arabia; **Verna Santos-Nafrada**, King Saud University, Saudi Arabia; **Gamal Abdelfattah Shehata**, Taibah University, Saudi Arabia; **Ron Stefan**, Institute of Public Administration, Saudi Arabia; **Dr. Saad Torki**, Imam Abdulrahman Bin Faisal University, Dammam, Saudi Arabia; **Silvia Yafai**, Applied Technology High School/Secondary Technical School, UAE; **Mahmood Zar**, Taibah University, Saudi Arabia; **Thouraya Zheni**, Taibah University, Saudi Arabia

Turkey

Sema Babacan, Istanbul Medipol University; **Bilge Çöllüoğlu Yakar**, Bilkent University; **Liana Corniel**, Koc University; **Savas Geylanioglu**, Izmir Bahcesehir Science and Technology College; **Öznur Güler**, Giresun University; **Selen Bilginer Halefoğlu**, Maltepe University; **Ahmet Konukoğlu**, Hasan Kalyoncu University; **Mehmet Salih Yoğun**, Gaziantep Hasan Kalyoncu University; **Fatih Yücel**, Beykent University

Europe

Irina Gerasimova, Saint-Petersburg Mining University, Russia; **Amina Al Hashamia**, University of Exeter, UK; **Jodi**, Las Dominicas, Spain; **Marina Khanykova**, School 179, Russia; **Oksana Postnikova**, Lingua Practica, Russia; **Nina Vasilchenko**, Soho-Bridge Language School, Russia

Q: Skills for Success THIRD EDITION

CRITICAL THINKING

The unique critical thinking approach of the *Q: Skills for Success* series has been further enhanced in the Third Edition. New features help you analyze, synthesize, and develop your ideas.

Unit question
The thought-provoking unit questions engage you with the topic and provide a critical thinking framework for the unit.

UNIT QUESTION

What makes a good leader?

A. Discuss these questions with your classmates.

1. Have you ever been a leader? For example, have you ever been in charge of a group at school or been the captain of a sports team? If so, what challenges did you face as a leader?
2. Think of a leader you admire. What makes this person a good leader?

Analysis
You can discuss your opinion of each listening text and analyze how it changes your perspective on the unit question.

SAY WHAT YOU THINK

SYNTHESIZE Think about Listening 1, Listening 2, and the unit video as you discuss the questions.

1. The speakers suggest that the appearance of a product or a space can send a message. What message do you send by your own appearance and the appearance of your possessions?
2. Think about a time that you judged someone based on how he or she looked or organized things. Was your first impression right or wrong? Why?
3. How can colors help a person to be more organized? How could a productive messy person use color to find things more easily?

NEW! Critical Thinking Strategy with video
Each unit includes a Critical Thinking Strategy with activities to give you step-by-step guidance in critical analysis of texts. An accompanying instructional video (available on iQ Online) provides extra support and examples.

NEW! Bloom's Taxonomy
Pink activity headings integrate verbs from Bloom's Taxonomy to help you see how each activity develops critical thinking skills.

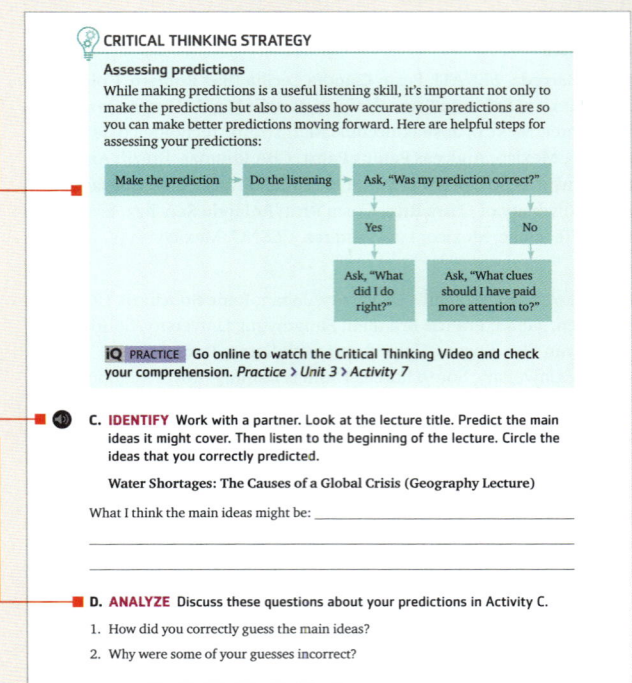

THREE TYPES OF VIDEO

UNIT VIDEO

The unit videos include high-interest documentaries and reports on a wide variety of subjects, all linked to the unit topic and question.

NEW! "Work with the Video" pages guide you in watching, understanding, and discussing the unit videos. The activities help you see the connection to the Unit Question and the other texts in the unit.

NEW! In some units, one of the main listening texts is a video.

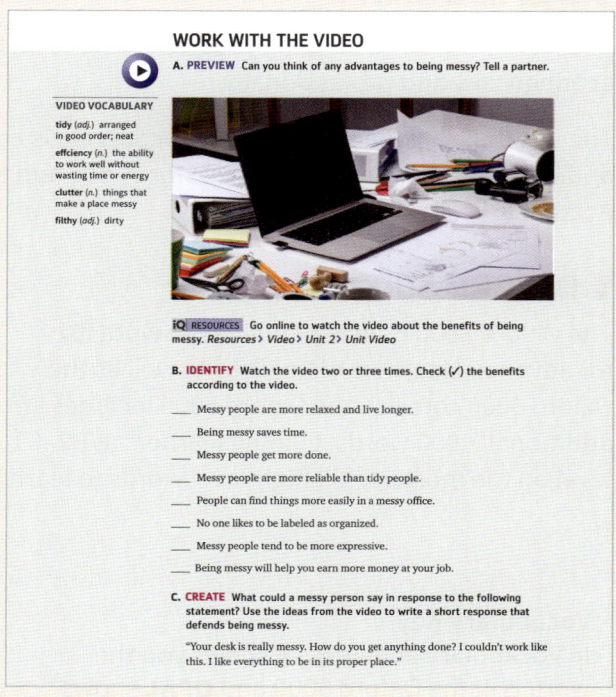

CRITICAL THINKING VIDEO

NEW! Narrated by the *Q* series authors, these short videos give you further instruction on the Critical Thinking Strategy of each unit using engaging images and graphics. You can use them to gain a deeper understanding of the Critical Thinking Strategy.

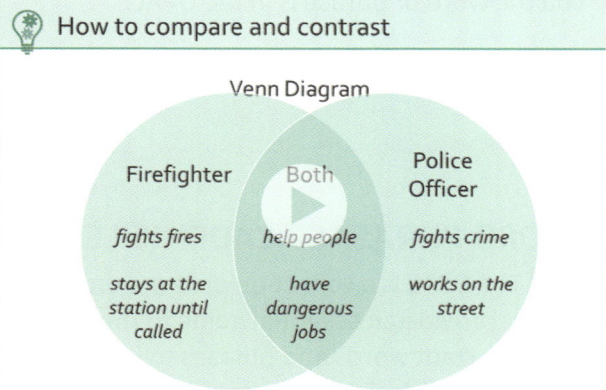

SKILLS VIDEO

NEW! These instructional videos provide illustrated explanations of skills and grammar points in the Student Book. They can be viewed in class or assigned for a flipped classroom, for homework, or for review. One skill video is available for every unit.

Easily access all videos in the Resources section of iQ Online.

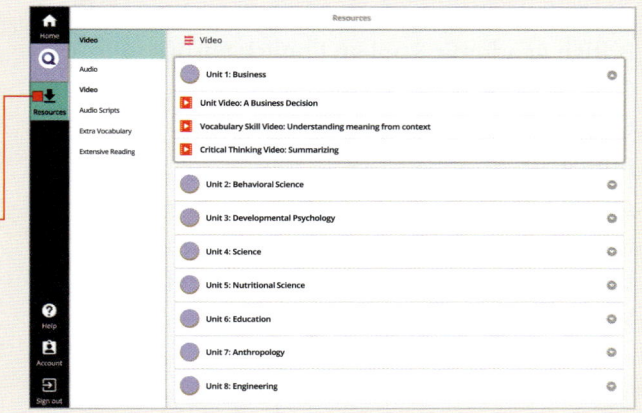

VOCABULARY

A research-based vocabulary program focuses on the words you need to know academically and professionally.

The vocabulary syllabus in *Q: Skills for Success* is correlated to the CEFR (see page 204) and linked to two word lists: the Oxford 5000 and the OPAL (Oxford Phrasal Academic Lexicon).

OXFORD 5000

The Oxford 5000 is an expanded core word list for advanced learners of English. As well as the Oxford 3000 core list, the Oxford 5000 includes an additional 2,000 words, guiding learners at B2–C1 level on the most useful, high-level words to learn.

> **Vocabulary Key**
> In vocabulary activities, 🔑 shows you the word is in the Oxford 5000 and **OPAL** shows you the word or phrase is in the OPAL.

OPAL
OXFORD PHRASAL ACADEMIC LEXICON

NEW! The OPAL is a collection of four word lists that provide an essential guide to the most important words and phrases to know for academic English. The word lists are based on the Oxford Corpus of Academic English and the British Academic Spoken English corpus. The OPAL includes both spoken and written academic English and both individual words and longer phrases.

Academic Language tips in the Student Book give information about how words and phrases from the OPAL are used and offer help with features such as collocations and phrases.

EXTENSIVE READING

NEW! Extensive Reading is a program of reading for pleasure at a level that matches your language ability.

There are many benefits to Extensive Reading:
- It helps you to become a better reader in general.
- It helps to increase your reading speed.
- It can improve your reading comprehension.
- It increases your vocabulary range.
- It can help you improve your grammar and writing skills.
- It's great for motivation to read something that is interesting for its own sake.

Each unit of *Q: Skills for Success* Third Edition has been aligned to an Oxford Graded Reader based on the appropriate topic and level of language proficiency. The first chapter of each recommended graded reader can be downloaded from iQ Online Resources.

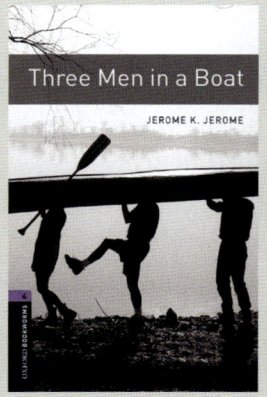
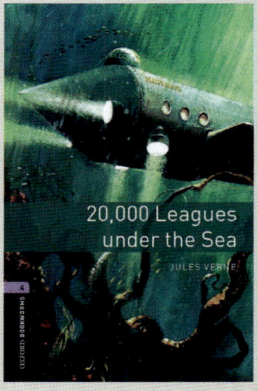
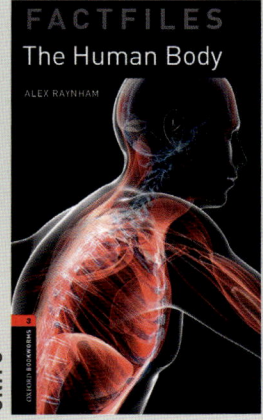
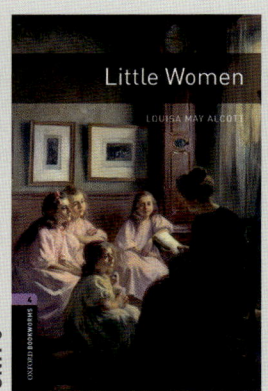
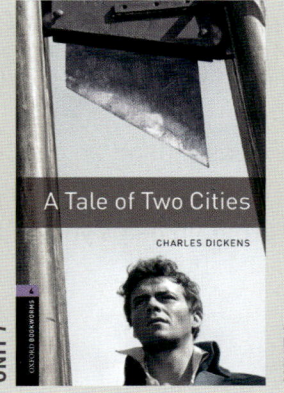

What is iQ ONLINE?

iQ ONLINE extends your learning beyond the classroom.

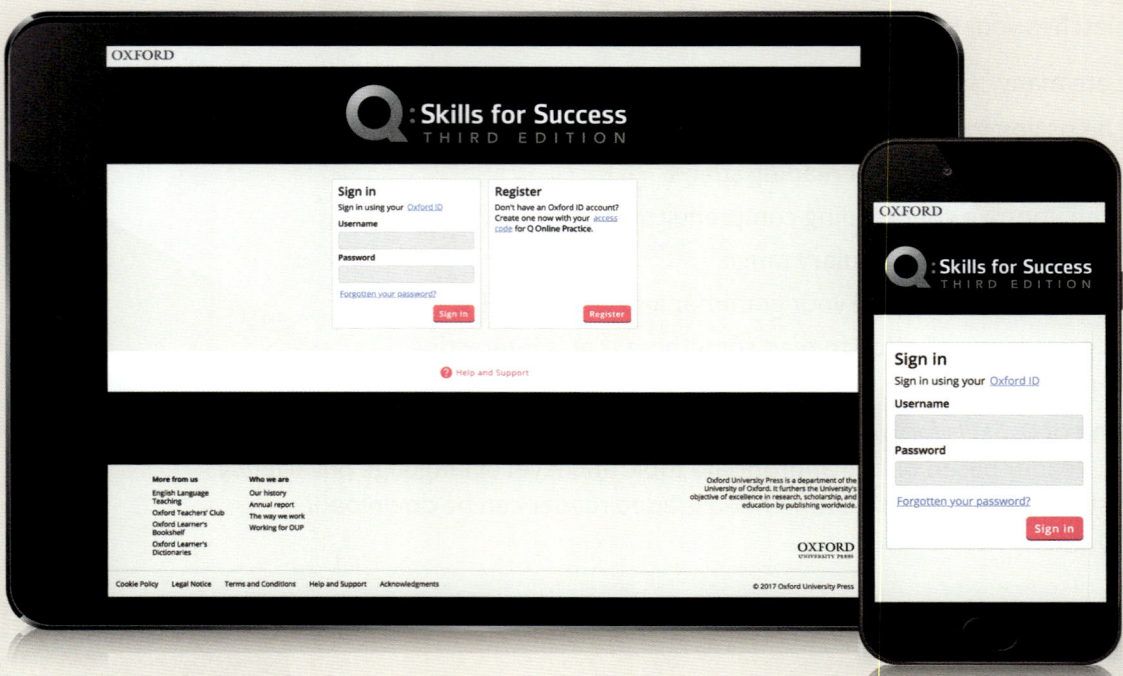

- Practice activities provide essential skills practice and support.
- Automatic grading and progress reports show you what you have mastered and where you need more practice.
- The Discussion Board allows you to discuss the Unit Questions and helps you develop your critical thinking.
- Essential resources such as audio and video are easy to access anytime.

NEW TO THE THIRD EDITION

- iQ Online is optimized for mobile use so you can use it on your phone.
- An updated interface allows easy navigation around the activities, tests, resources, and scores.
- New Critical Thinking Videos expand on the Critical Thinking Strategies in the Student Book.
- The Extensive Reading program helps you improve your vocabulary and reading skills.

How to use iQ ONLINE

Go to **Practice** to find additional practice and support to complement your learning in the classroom.

Go to **Resources** to find:
- All Student Book video
- All Student Book audio
- Critical Thinking videos
- Skills videos
- Extensive Reading

Go to **Messages** and **Discussion Board** to communicate with your teacher and classmates.

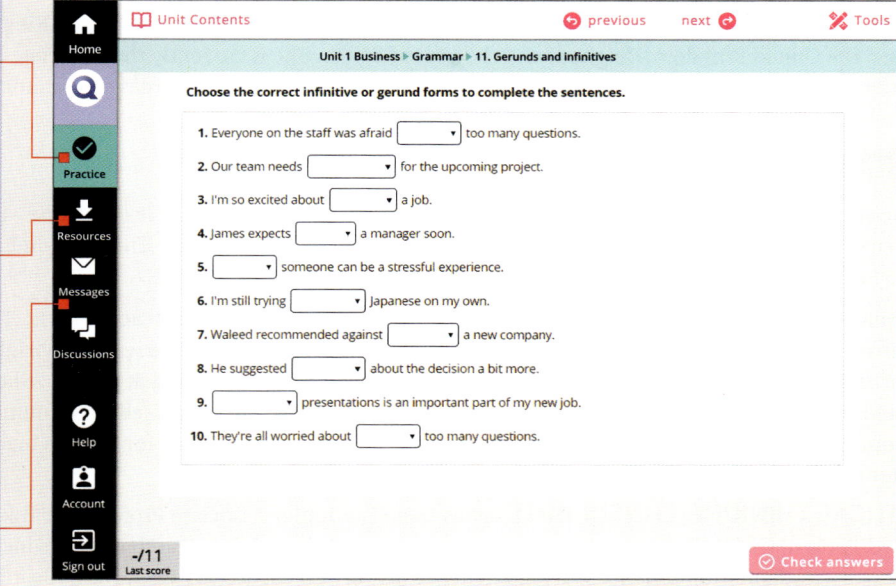

Online tests assigned by your teacher help you assess your progress and see where you need more practice.

A progress bar shows you how many activities you have completed.

View your scores for all activities.

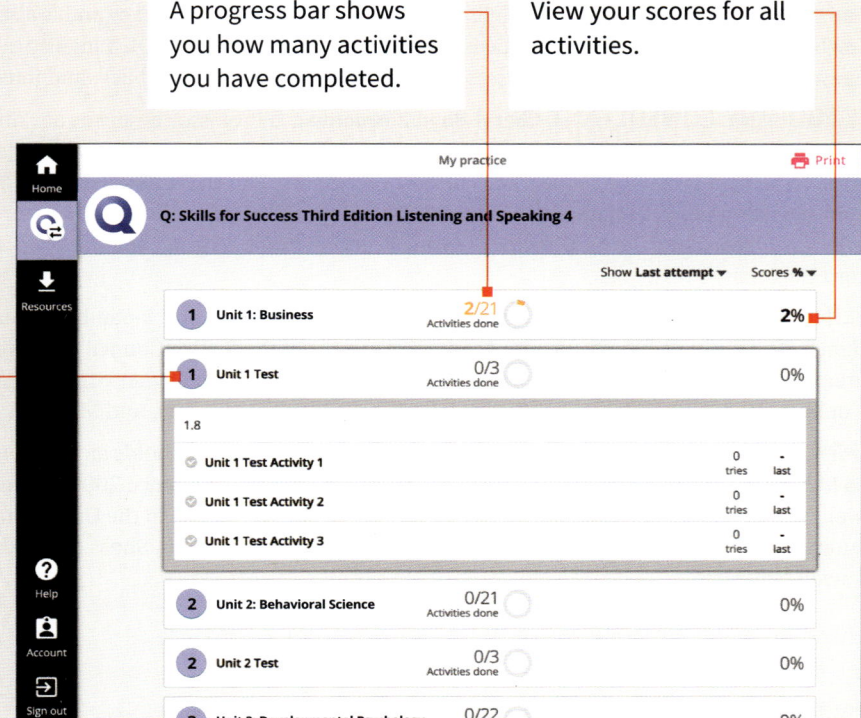

ix

AUTHORS AND CONSULTANTS

AUTHORS

Robert Freire holds an M.A. in Applied Linguistics from Montclair State University in New Jersey. He is a teacher and materials developer with more than ten years of ELT experience. He most recently taught ESL and linguistics at Montclair State University.

Tamara Jones holds a Ph.D. in Education from the University of Sheffield in the United Kingdom. She has taught in Russia, Korea, the United Kingdom, Belgium, and the United States. She is currently the Associate Director of the English Language Center at Howard Community College in Maryland. She specializes in the areas of pronunciation and conversation.

SERIES CONSULTANTS

Lawrence J. Zwier holds an M.A. in TESL from the University of Minnesota. He is currently the Associate Director for Curriculum Development at the English Language Center at Michigan State University in East Lansing. He has taught ESL/EFL in the United States, Saudi Arabia, Malaysia, Japan, and Singapore.

Marguerite Ann Snow holds a Ph.D. in Applied Linguistics from UCLA. She teaches in the TESOL M.A. program in the Charter College of Education at California State University, Los Angeles. She was a Fulbright scholar in Hong Kong and Cyprus. In 2006, she received the President's Distinguished Professor award at CSULA. She has trained ESL teachers in the United States and EFL teachers in more than 25 countries. She is the author/editor of numerous publications in the areas of content-based instruction, English for academic purposes, and standards for English teaching and learning. She is a co-editor of *Teaching English as a Second or Foreign Language* (4th ed.).

CRITICAL THINKING CONSULTANT **James Dunn** is a Junior Associate Professor at Tokai University and the Coordinator of the JALT Critical Thinking Special Interest Group. His research interests include critical thinking skills' impact on student brain function during English learning as measured by EEG. His educational goals are to help students understand that they are capable of more than they might think and to expand their cultural competence with critical thinking and higher-order thinking skills.

ASSESSMENT CONSULTANT **Elaine Boyd** has worked in assessment for over 30 years for international testing organizations. She has designed and delivered courses in assessment literacy and is also the author of several EL exam coursebooks for leading publishers. She is an Associate Tutor (M.A. TESOL/Linguistics) at University College, London. Her research interests are classroom assessment, issues in managing feedback, and intercultural competences.

VOCABULARY CONSULTANT **Cheryl Boyd Zimmerman** is Professor Emeritus at California State University, Fullerton. She specialized in second-language vocabulary acquisition, an area in which she is widely published. She taught graduate courses on second-language acquisition, culture, vocabulary, and the fundamentals of TESOL, and has been a frequent invited speaker on topics related to vocabulary teaching and learning. She is the author of *Word Knowledge: A Vocabulary Teacher's Handbook* and Series Director of *Inside Reading, Inside Writing,* and *Inside Listening and Speaking,* published by Oxford University Press.

ONLINE INTEGRATION **Chantal Hemmi** holds an Ed.D. TEFL and is a Japan-based teacher trainer and curriculum designer. Since leaving her position as Academic Director of the British Council in Tokyo, she has been teaching at the Center for Language Education and Research at Sophia University in an EAP/CLIL program offered for undergraduates. She delivers lectures and teacher trainings throughout Japan, Indonesia, and Malaysia.

COMMUNICATIVE GRAMMAR CONSULTANT **Nancy Schoenfeld** holds an M.A. in TESOL from Biola University in La Mirada, California, and has been an English language instructor since 2000. She has taught ESL in California and Hawaii, and EFL in Thailand and Kuwait. She has also trained teachers in the United States and Indonesia. Her interests include teaching vocabulary, extensive reading, and student motivation. She is currently an English Language Instructor at Kuwait University.

CONTENTS

Welcome to *Q: Skills for Success* Third Edition iv
What is iQ Online? viii
Authors and Consultants x

UNIT 5 Nutritional Science – How has science changed the food we eat? 102
- Note-taking Skill: Editing notes after a lecture 104
- Listening 1 (Video): Improving Farming with Flying Robots 105
- Listening Skill: Understanding bias in a presentation 109
- Listening 2: The Science Behind Food Cravings 110
- Critical Thinking Strategy: Evaluating information 115
- Vocabulary Skill: Prefixes and suffixes 116
- Grammar: Comparative forms of adjectives and adverbs 118
- Pronunciation: Common intonation patterns 120
- Speaking Skill: Expressing interest during a conversation 121
- Unit Assignment: Take part in a debate 123

UNIT 6 Education – Is one road to success better than another? 126
- Note-taking Skill: Comparing and contrasting multiple topics 128
- Listening 1 (Video): Failure and Success in Startups 129
- Listening Skill: Listening for contrasting ideas 133
- Listening 2: Interns in New York 134
- Critical Thinking Strategy: Ranking options 139
- Vocabulary Skill: Using the dictionary: formal and informal words 140
- Grammar: Simple, compound, and complex sentences 142
- Pronunciation: Highlighted words 144
- Speaking Skill: Changing the topic 146
- Unit Assignment: Reach a group decision 147

UNIT 7 Anthropology – How can accidental discoveries affect our lives? 152
- Listening 1: The Power of Serendipity 154
- Listening Skill: Listening for signal words and phrases 158
- Note-taking Skill: Taking notes on details 160
- Listening 2: Against All Odds, Twin Girls Reunited 162
- Work with the Video: Phineas Gage 166
- Vocabulary Skill: Collocations with prepositions 167
- Grammar: Indirect speech 169
- Pronunciation: Linked words with vowels 171
- Speaking Skill: Using questions to maintain listener interest 172
- Critical Thinking Strategy: Combining ideas 174
- Unit Assignment: Tell a story 175

UNIT 8 Engineering – What are the consequences of progress? 178
- Listening 1: Automation and Us 180
- Listening Skill: Listening for causes and effects 185
- Note-taking Skill: Taking notes on causes and effects 187
- Listening 2: Driverless Cars 188
- Critical Thinking Strategy: Making appraisals 193
- Work with the Video: Driverless Trucks 194
- Vocabulary Skill: Idioms 196
- Grammar: Real conditionals 197
- Pronunciation: Thought groups 199
- Speaking Skill: Adding to another speaker's comments 200
- Unit Assignment: Share opinions about the consequences of progress 201

Vocabulary List and CEFR Correlation 204

Nutritional Science

NOTE-TAKING	editing notes after a lecture
LISTENING	understanding bias in a presentation
CRITICAL THINKING	evaluating information
VOCABULARY	prefixes and suffixes
GRAMMAR	comparative forms of adjectives and adverbs
PRONUNCIATION	common intonation patterns
SPEAKING	expressing interest during a conversation

UNIT QUESTION

How has science changed the food we eat?

A. Discuss these questions with your classmates.

1. Which is most important in the food you choose: flavor, cost, or nutrition? Why?
2. How does TV advertising affect what food you eat?
3. Look at the photo. What is the person doing? Would you eat food grown in this field? Why or why not?

B. Listen to *The Q Classroom* online. Then answer these questions.

1. Yuna says packaged food is good for us because it has more vitamins and less fat. Felix and Marcus state that packaged food is not healthy. Who do you agree with? Why?
2. Sophy says that because of science, we can grow bigger plants and animals. What might be an advantage to having bigger food?

iQ PRACTICE Go to the online discussion board to discuss the Unit Question with your classmates. *Practice > Unit 5 > Activity 1*

UNIT OBJECTIVE ▶ Watch a video and listen to a radio report and gather information and ideas to participate in a debate on food science.

NOTE-TAKING SKILL Editing notes after a lecture

In order to remember most of what you hear, it is a good idea to review your notes within 24 hours after a lecture. As you read your notes, annotate them (add notes to a text, giving explanations or comments):

1. Underline or highlight key ideas.
2. Cross out information that isn't important.
3. Use the extra space on the paper to add your thoughts and make connections between the lecture and the information in your textbook.
4. Use a dictionary to look up all new key words. Write the definition or translation.
5. Make notes about what you don't understand so you can ask your teacher later.
6. Add a short summary of your notes.

A. APPLY Listen to the lecture about food as medicine. Then edit the notes based on the first four annotation tips above. Compare your edits with a partner.

Peking duck

Using food in place of medicine

1. China—Peking duck
   a. Famous and delicious
   b. Red rice powder on duck skin
   c. Lowers cholesterol (?)
   d. Fewer Chinese people get heart disease than other countries
2. Brazil—Hammerhead shark liver oil
   a. Indigenous (native) populations off the coast of Brazil
   b. Cure asthma (trouble breathing)
   c. Endangered (?)
   d. Now, researchers are testing asthma drugs made from oil from nurse & blue sharks

shark liver oil

B. COMPOSE Review the notes again. Write two follow-up questions and a short summary based on the fifth and sixth annotation tips above. Share your summary with a partner.

iQ PRACTICE Go online for more practice editing notes after a lecture.
Practice > Unit 5 > Activity 2

LISTENING

LISTENING 1 **Improving Farming with Flying Robots**

OBJECTIVE ▶ You are going to watch a video news report about how technology can help farmers. As you watch, gather information and ideas about how the use of drones, or flying robots, might change the food we eat.

PREVIEW THE LISTENING

A. PREVIEW Discuss the questions in a small group.

1. Farming can be a difficult job. What problems do you think farmers might face today?

2. How do you think technology like drones might help farmers? What can drones do to make farming easier and more efficient?

B. VOCABULARY Read aloud these words from Listening 1. Check (✓) the ones you know. Use a dictionary to define any new or unknown words. Then discuss with a partner how the words will relate to the unit.

buzz *(v.)*	infection *(n.)* 🔑	revolution *(n.)* 🔑
distribute *(v.)* 🔑 OPAL	load *(n.)* 🔑	suffer *(v.)* 🔑
dominate *(v.)* 🔑 OPAL	precision *(n.)* 🔑 OPAL	survey *(n.)* 🔑 OPAL
ignorance *(n.)* 🔑	productivity *(n.)* 🔑	

🔑 Oxford 5000™ words   **OPAL** Oxford Phrasal Academic Lexicon

iQ PRACTICE Go online to listen and practice your pronunciation.
Practice > Unit 5 > Activity 3

WORK WITH THE LISTENING

iQ RESOURCES Go online to watch the video.
Resources > Video > Unit 5 > Listening 1

 A. LISTEN AND TAKE NOTES Watch the video.* Read the student's notes about how farmers can use drones. Match the note headings with the correct rows.

iQ RESOURCES Go online to download extra vocabulary support.
Resources > Extra Vocabulary > Unit 5

Concerns about using robots	Possible uses for drones	Pressures on farmers
	too hard to use not reliable enough too expensive we think of drones as military weapons	
	feed more people lower the chemical load use less water farms are bigger than before fewer workers on the farms crops can get disease/infections	
	get data measure their farms look for disease they can see if chemicals should be sprayed on the crops	

B. IDENTIFY Edit the notes. Underline or highlight key words and phrases and cross out words that are not important. Also, explain or define new vocabulary and make notes about what you still don't understand.

C. DISCUSS Work with a partner. Use your notes to summarize the information in the video. Answer the questions.

1. Why are people concerned about using robots?
2. What pressures do farmers face today?
3. How could farmers use drones?

* Audio version available. *Resources > Audio > Unit 5*

D. IDENTIFY Watch the video again. Check (✓) the main ideas mentioned in the report.

☐ 1. Drones are the future of aviation.
☐ 2. Drones can help farmers feed more people.
☐ 3. Farms are getting bigger and bigger.
☐ 4. Farmers can use drones to get big data on their crops.
☐ 5. Farmers have to spray their crops to fight disease.
☐ 6. Cows are milked by milking machines nowadays.
☐ 7. Farming is the biggest industry in the world.
☐ 8. Drones are not weapons.

E. INTERPRET Read the comments below. Do you think the farmers would be more likely to use drone technology on their farms or less likely? Write *ML* (more likely) or *LL* (less likely).

_____ 1. "I have a real problem getting to all the parts of my farm. It's huge, and I don't have time to drive around it as often as I should."

_____ 2. "I'm not sure using a drone is safe. What happens to the data it records? Would other farmers be able to get information about my crops?"

_____ 3. "We bought our farm as a change from city living. We produce small batches of high-quality goat cheese. Our goats are like family members."

_____ 4. "I love how technology makes farming easier. I have a GPS-guided planting system and sensors that tell us where to water."

_____ 5. "Drones are expensive, and changes in the weather have caused our crops to fail the past two years. We don't have extra money for technology."

_____ 6. "I need a way to reduce the amount of chemicals I use to keep my crops healthy. I often overspray because I can't get good data on my plants."

F. VOCABULARY Here are some words from Listening 1. Read the sentences. Then write each bold word next to the correct definition.

1. I hate to admit my **ignorance**, but I don't know anything about this topic.
2. The money was **distributed** evenly to each person who won.
3. You can put your **load** of laundry in the washing machine.
4. She **dominated** the conversation by talking a lot and not letting anyone else speak.

ACADEMIC LANGUAGE

Vocabulary can often be learned in word forms. For example, *precision* is a noun. The adjective form is *precise*, and the adverb form is *precisely*. You can use any of the forms to mean exact, accurate, and careful.

| OPAL
Oxford Phrasal Academic Lexicon

5. It is important that surgeons operate with **precision**. If they are not careful, they might hurt their patients.
6. The social media **revolution** changed the way we interact with our friends.
7. I **suffer** from leg pains at night, so I am going to talk to my doctor.
8. He read a **survey** of the country's history to increase his general knowledge about it.
9. Can you please turn off your phone so it doesn't **buzz** in the meeting?
10. He looked at the trees to find any sign of **infection** that would show the trees were sick.
11. How much you are paid depends on your **productivity**.

a. _____ (*n.*) the quality of being exact, accurate, and careful

b. _____ (*n.*) the total amount that something can carry or contain

c. _____ (*n.*) a great change in conditions, ways of working, beliefs, etc., that affects large numbers of people

d. _____ (*v.*) to make a sound like a bee

e. _____ (*v.*) to control or have a lot of influence over somebody/something

f. _____ (*n.*) the rate at which a worker, a company, or a country produces goods

g. _____ (*n.*) a lack of knowledge or information about something

h. _____ (*n.*) an illness that is caused by bacteria or a virus

i. _____ (*v.*) to be badly affected by a disease, pain, sadness, a lack of something, etc.

j. _____ (*v.*) to share between a number of people

k. _____ (*n.*) a general study, view, or description of something

iQ PRACTICE Go online for more practice with the vocabulary.
Practice > Unit 5 > Activity 4

iQ PRACTICE Go online for additional listening and comprehension.
Practice > Unit 5 > Activity 5

SAY WHAT YOU THINK

DISCUSS Work in a group to discuss the questions.

1. The scientist in the report says that his job "is to make [drones] cheap and easy and ubiquitous, and then ultimately the users figure out what the application is for." What do you think this means? Do you agree or disagree that this is a good way to do things? Why?

2. Do you think using drones on farms is a good idea? Why?

LISTENING SKILL Understanding bias in a presentation

Bias is a strong feeling for or against something. Understanding the bias in a presentation is important. Speakers may express biases even when they're trying to sound objective. In Listening 1, the speaker mentions some problems with using drones on farms, but the speaker's bias appears to be in favor of technology and farming.

There are several clues to help you understand the bias of a presentation.

Title: Listening 1 is called "Improving Farming with Flying Robots." This is a positive idea, and it sounds very definite. This probably means the video is in favor of using drones in farming. A different title, such as "Some Farmers Believe That Drones May Increase Food Production," does not show such a strong bias.

Introduction: Pay attention to how a speaker introduces a topic. For example, if a speaker starts with, *I'm going to talk about all the benefits to using technology on farms*, that statement alone tells you the speaker's bias.

Imbalance: Presentations with a bias usually report on both sides of the issue, but the information is not balanced well. In Listening 1, most of the video is about how drones can help farmers, and only a small part of the video is about the possible problems of using drones.

Information source: Consider who is providing the information. For example, suppose a company that manufactures drones paid for this report. Knowing that the company makes drones can help you decide how much to trust the information.

 A. IDENTIFY Listen to the short report. Then answer the questions.

1. Check (✓) the clues you hear that tell you the bias.
   - ☐ Title
   - ☐ Introduction
   - ☐ Imbalance
   - ☐ Information source

2. Is the speaker against or in favor of organic food?

B. IDENTIFY Listen to excerpts from four news reports. What bias is being shown in each report? Circle the correct answers.

Excerpt 1

a. Some scientists believe there are many causes of obesity.

b. Some scientists believe fast food is a main cause of obesity.

Excerpt 2

a. Drinking soda may cause heart disease.

b. Drinking soda is part of a healthy lifestyle.

Excerpt 3

a. Drinking too much tea can be harmful.

b. Drinking tea is an old tradition.

Excerpt 4

a. Food labels can help us make good choices.

b. Food labels can be difficult to believe.

iQ PRACTICE Go online for more practice listening to understand bias in a presentation. *Practice > Unit 5 > Activity 6*

LISTENING 2 The Science Behind Food Cravings

OBJECTIVE ▶

You are going to listen to a radio report about food cravings. A *food craving* is a strong desire to eat a specific food. Scientists disagree about why people get these food cravings. As you listen to the report, gather information and ideas about how science affects the food we eat.

PREVIEW THE LISTENING

A. PREVIEW What kinds of food do you crave? Do you usually give in to your craving and eat the food or not? Discuss with a partner.

B. VOCABULARY Read aloud these words from Listening 2. Check (✓) the ones you know. Use a dictionary to define any new or unknown words. Then discuss with a partner how the words will relate to the unit.

alter (v.) OPAL	disturbing (adj.)	reaction (n.) OPAL
compound (v.)	ethics (n.) OPAL	ultimate (adj.) OPAL
consumer (n.)	intense (adj.)	
debate (n.) OPAL	modification (n.)	

Oxford 5000™ words   OPAL Oxford Phrasal Academic Lexicon

iQ PRACTICE Go online to listen and practice your pronunciation.
Practice > Unit 5 > Activity 7

WORK WITH THE LISTENING

A. LISTEN AND TAKE NOTES Listen to the radio report. Complete the notes on the speakers and their comments.

Speaker	Job	Comments
Lara Jones	nutritionist	• food cravings affect _____ • might be message from body signaling _____ chips craving = _____ chocolate craving = _____
Dr. Svacina	dietary psychologist	• disagrees → we don't crave all foods high in magnesium (e.g., _____, _____) • cravings can come from _____ • _____ also affects cravings Americans → _____ Egyptians → _____
Howazen Al Ganem	professor of ethics in advertising	• TV images of _____ cause cravings • need to think about ethics of _____ • adults can change _____

LISTENING 2

B. **DISCUSS** Compare your notes with a partner. Whose comments and opinions do you think are more likely to be true? Why? Have any of the speakers changed the way you think about food cravings?

C. **IDENTIFY** Listen to the radio report again. Circle the correct answers.

1. In general, the panel of experts on the radio show agree that _____.

    a. the problem of food cravings affects most people

    b. the cause of food cravings is clear

    c. food cravings are biological

2. According to the radio report, _____.

    a. people should eat more junk food

    b. food cravings are never the result of a need for a nutrient

    c. food cravings may be caused by certain feelings

3. According to the report, TV viewers should probably _____.

    a. stop watching TV with their children

    b. walk away when the food advertisements come on

    c. change the laws to end food advertising

4. In general, the speakers _____ of food cravings.

    a. completely explained the causes

    b. didn't explain any of the causes

    c. explained some possible causes

112   UNIT 5   How has science changed the food we eat?

D. CATEGORIZE Read the statements. Write *T* (true) or *F* (false). Then correct each false statement to make it true.

____ 1. Food cravings usually appear quickly and without warning.

____ 2. According to some nutritionists, a food craving is caused by having too much of a particular nutrient.

____ 3. Some scientists believe that food cravings come from positive emotions.

____ 4. Sometimes we only crave a kind of food because we see it around us or on TV.

____ 5. Eating a little bit of the food we crave can make the craving disappear.

E. EVALUATE Read the comments below. Which of the speakers from the radio report would be most likely to say them? Match the speaker with the comment.

____ 1. The radio show host

____ 2. Dr. Svacina, a dietary psychologist

____ 3. Lara Jones, a nutritionist

____ 4. Howazen Al Ganem, a professor of ethics in advertising

a. "A person who craves cheese may need more omega-3 fatty acids in their body. Instead of eating cheese, the person could eat walnuts or salmon. These are healthier choices and contain high levels of this nutrient."

b. "Recent research has shown us that children see a lot of TV advertisements for fast food. One study found that American preschoolers saw 2.8 fast-food ads on TV every day in 2012. That means children may be experiencing junk food cravings now more than ever before."

c. "Doing things to reduce the stress you have in your life might also reduce your food cravings. Try to do some yoga, take a walk, or call a friend. Feeling calmer may result in fewer trips to the refrigerator."

d. "I am glad to know that I am not alone in my food cravings. It appears that many other people have the same cravings. The key for me will be to limit myself to a healthy amount when I really feel like eating a whole bar or bag."

F. DISCUSS Work in a group to discuss the questions.

1. Advertisers use images of food to convince you to buy their product. Can you think of an advertisement you have seen that was very effective? What was the food, and why might the advertisement trigger a food craving?

2. Some experts suggest eating a little bit of the food you crave in order to stop the craving. Do you think this is good advice? Why or why not? What other things can people do to overcome food cravings?

VOCABULARY SKILL REVIEW

In Unit 4, you learned about word forms. Try to find different word forms for the following vocabulary words in Activity G: *consumer, disturbing, ethics, modification, reaction*. Use a dictionary to help you.

G. VOCABULARY Here are some words from Listening 2. Complete each sentence with the correct word.

alter (v.)	debate (n.)	intense (adj.)	reaction (n.)
compound (v.)	disturbing (adj.)	modification (n.)	ultimate (adj.)
consumer (n.)	ethics (n.)		

1. I don't eat enough vegetables. To _____ the problem, my grocery store does not have much fresh produce.

2. I get _____ headaches. They are very strong.

3. I find it very _____ that people eat so much processed food. How can they eat that stuff instead of fruits and vegetables?

4. Advertisers try to catch the interest of any _____ who will want to buy their products.

5. When they said the newly created carrots were bright red, my first _____ was to say I didn't believe it.

6. We need to _____ our diet. I want to reduce the amount of processed food we eat.

7. Some people wanted the new factory in their town and some didn't. The _____ over building the new factory went on for years.

8. I think a bowl of ice cream with whipped cream is the _____ dessert. Nothing could be better than that!

9. I question the _____ of creating "superfoods." I'm not sure I agree that genetic engineering is always good.

10. This corn is very similar to normal corn, but scientists made a small _____ to its genes that makes it resist disease.

iQ PRACTICE Go online for more practice with the vocabulary.
Practice > Unit 5 > Activity 8

CRITICAL THINKING STRATEGY

Evaluating information

We can't believe everything we hear. **Evaluating information** is an important part of thinking critically. One step in evaluating information is identifying speaker bias, which you learned about in the Listening Skill. We need to think about who the speaker is and if he or she is a real expert on the subject. Another step is listening for the speaker to provide proof. We can also compare what we hear to our own experience.

iQ PRACTICE Go online to watch the Critical Thinking Video and check your comprehension. *Practice > Unit 5 > Activity 9*

H. EVALUATE Listen to the speakers. Complete the checklist evaluating the information each speaker shares.

	Speaker 1	Speaker 2	Speaker 3
The speaker is not biased.	☐	☐	☐
The speaker is an expert.	☐	☐	☐
The speaker provides proof.	☐	☐	☐
The speaker's ideas agree with my life experience.	☐	☐	☐

I. RESTATE Do you believe the speakers? Why or why not? Listen again. Complete the sentences with evidence in the speakers' words. Then share your opinions and reasons with a partner.

Speaker 1	I believe / don't believe the speaker because . . .
Speaker 2	I believe / don't believe the speaker because . . .
Speaker 3	I believe / don't believe the speaker because . . .

SAY WHAT YOU THINK

SYNTHESIZE Think about Listening 1 and Listening 2 as you discuss the questions.

1. Listening 1 described how farmers might use science to grow more food. Listening 2 is about how science can explain our eating habits. Which research were you most interested in? Which is more important for your life? For the world? Why?

2. Listening 1 was one expert's presentation. Listening 2 was a conversation among three experts. Do you prefer to get information from one source or from a conversation among several sources? How do you prefer to hear information?

VOCABULARY SKILL Prefixes and suffixes

Prefixes

Adding a **prefix** to the beginning of a word changes the meaning of the word. Understanding a prefix can help you identify the meaning of a word.

Prefix	Meaning	Example
dis-	opposite of	disorders
under-	less than enough	underdeveloped
re-	again	rebound
un-	not	uneasy

Suffixes

Adding a suffix to the end of a word often changes the part of speech. For example, adding *-ly* to the adjective *wide* changes the word to the adverb *widely*.

Suffix	Meaning	Example
-al, -ic	(*adj.*) about, connected with	chemical, genetic
-(at)ion	(*n.*) a state or process	reaction
-ist	(*n.*) a person who does	scientist
-less	(*adj.*) not having something	seedless
-(al)ly	(*adv.*) in a particular way	genetically
-ness	(*n.*) a quality	freshness

TIP FOR SUCCESS

Many words drop letters before a suffix is added. Look in the dictionary to see if there are spelling changes when adding suffixes to a word.

A. APPLY Write the meaning of each word. Look at the prefixes in the chart on page 116 to help you.

1. disapprove _____
2. redo _____
3. unfair _____
4. underfeed _____
5. untie _____
6. dislike _____

B. APPLY Look at the words and phrases below. Write the correct form of the word. Use the suffixes in the chart on page 116 to help you.

1. science (*n.* person) _scientist_
2. origin (*adv.*) _____
3. unique (*n.* quality) _____
4. no weight (*adj.*) _____
5. about a topic (*adj.*) _____
6. relate (*n.*) _____

C. COMPOSE Choose five words from Activities A and B. Write a sentence for each word. Then take turns reading your sentences to a partner.

iQ PRACTICE Go online for more practice using prefixes and suffixes.
Practice > Unit 5 > Activity 10

SPEAKING

OBJECTIVE ▶ At the end of this unit, you are going to participate in a debate on food science, stating and supporting your opinions about food modification. During the debate, you will need to be able to use comparative forms of adjectives and adverbs and express interest in a conversation.

GRAMMAR Comparative forms of adjectives and adverbs

Comparative forms of adjectives and adverbs compare two things or actions. The rules for making comparatives are similar for both adjectives and adverbs.

Condition	Rule	Example
one-syllable adjectives	add -er	older
one-syllable adverbs		faster
one-syllable adjectives ending in -e	add -r	nicer
two-syllable adjectives ending in -y	change the y to i and add -er	healthier
most other adjectives	use more or less before the word	more interesting
all other adverbs		less naturally

Some adjectives take either -er or more.

narrow	→	narrower, more narrow
simple	→	simpler, more simple
quiet	→	quieter, more quiet
gentle	→	gentler, more gentle
handsome	→	handsomer, more handsome

Some adjectives and adverbs are irregular. This means the comparative adjective and adverb forms are not based on the base forms.

good	→	better	badly	→	worse
well	→	better	far	→	farther / further
bad	→	worse	little	→	less

To compare things or actions, use the word *than* after the comparative adjective or adverb.

Vegetables are healthier **than** junk food.

Many people are concerned about eating more healthfully **than** they were in the past.

iQ RESOURCES Go online to watch the Grammar Skill Video.
Resources > Video > Unit 5 > Grammar Skill Video

A. APPLY Write the comparative forms of the adjectives and adverbs. Then work with a partner. Take turns saying sentences using these comparative forms.

1. flavorful _____
2. uneasy _____
3. high _____
4. tasty _____
5. widely _____
6. unnatural _____
7. acceptable _____
8. bad _____
9. loyal _____
10. expensive _____

B. CREATE Work with a partner. Take turns asking and answering comparative questions.

Example: ice cream / delicious / chocolate / strawberry

A: Which kind of ice cream do you think is more delicious, chocolate or strawberry?
B: I think strawberry ice cream is more delicious than chocolate ice cream.

1. juice / sweet / pineapple / orange
2. peach / flavorful / preserved / fresh
3. TV show / disturbing / the news / reality TV
4. drink / widely enjoyed / tea / coffee
5. food / expensive / organic / genetically engineered

iQ PRACTICE Go online for more practice with comparative forms of adjectives and adverbs. *Practice > Unit 5 > Activity 11*

iQ PRACTICE Go online for the Grammar Expansion: *So . . . that* and *such (an) . . . that*. *Practice > Unit 5 > Activity 12*

PRONUNCIATION Common intonation patterns

Intonation is an important part of communicating your ideas. There are common intonation patterns for specific conversational actions. Make sure you are using the correct pattern to help express your meaning.

To ask for clarification, use a rising intonation.

> This tomato is genetically altered?
> **Meaning:** I am not sure I heard you, or I am not sure I understand you.

To express surprise, use a rising intonation.

> You eat five sandwiches a day?
> **Meaning:** I am surprised by this information.

To list items, use a rising intonation for each item on the list. For the last item, use a rising/falling intonation.

> I ate eggs, toast, and cereal.
> **Meaning:** I ate these three things.

For *yes/no* questions, use a rising intonation.

> Would you like coffee?
> **Meaning:** You can say *yes* or *no* to my question.

To offer a choice between two things, use a rising/falling intonation.

> Would you like coffee or iced tea?
> **Meaning:** Which would you prefer?

A. APPLY Listen to the sentences. Draw intonation arrows over each one. Then practice saying the sentences with a partner.

1. What? You've never eaten a tomato?
2. Do you prefer water or juice?
3. My favorite foods are rice, yams, and pizza.
4. What did you say? You don't like ice cream?
5. Are you hungry? Do you want some bread and cheese?

TIP FOR SUCCESS

When you listen to the radio, focus on the speakers' intonation. Pay attention to how they use their voices to express ideas and emotions.

B. DISCUSS Work with a partner. Take turns asking and answering the questions. Ask follow-up questions if needed. Focus on using the correct intonation.

1. What are your favorite foods?
2. What are three foods you would never try?
3. Who usually cooks at your house?

iQ PRACTICE Go online for more practice with common intonation patterns. *Practice > Unit 5 > Activity 13*

SPEAKING SKILL Expressing interest during a conversation

Expressing interest during a conversation shows the speaker you are paying attention. There are several ways to express interest in the speaker's ideas. In addition to leaning forward and making eye contact, you can use special words and phrases to show you are interested.

Encouraging words: Yeah. / Wow! / Mm-hmm. / Cool!
Comments: How interesting! / That's amazing!
Emphasis questions: Really?
Repeating words: Speaker: I went to Paris. You: Oh, Paris!

It is not necessary to wait until the speaker has finished talking to use these words and phrases. You can use them throughout the conversation, whenever the speaker completes a thought.

A. APPLY Listen to the conversation between two students who are eating lunch. Fill in the blanks with the words and phrases in the box. Then practice the conversation with a partner.

| every day | really | wow |
| mm-hmm | that's interesting | yeah |

Faisal: Hey, Marc. Is this seat free? Do you mind if I sit here?

Marc: Not at all. How are you doing?

Faisal: I'm absolutely starving!

Marc: _____1_____? Why?

Faisal: I went to the gym this morning before school, and by 11:00, my stomach was growling in class.

Marc: _____2, that had to be embarrassing.

Faisal: Definitely. So, what did you get for lunch?

Marc: Well, they're serving French onion soup today, so I got some of that. It's not bad, but not like home!

Faisal: _____3! French food is famous around the world, but I've never had it.

Marc: Well, I am from Provence, in the south of France. People take food very seriously there.

Faisal: _____4.

Marc: People buy fresh fruit and vegetables from the market every day.

Faisal: _____5?

Marc: Yeah, and the cheese is amazing! It tastes nothing like what we buy in the grocery stores here.

Faisal: _____6. I feel that way about Saudi Arabian food here, too. It's not quite the same.

B. DISCUSS Work in a group to answer the questions. As you listen, use different ways to express interest and show you are paying attention.

1. What food or drink would you recommend to someone who has a cold? Are there any traditional remedies you use in your family?

2. Which meal is the most important of the day to you? Why?

3. Can you cook? If so, what is a dish that you make particularly well? How do you make it?

iQ PRACTICE Go online for more practice expressing interest during a conversation. *Practice > Unit 5 > Activity 14*

UNIT ASSIGNMENT Take part in a debate

OBJECTIVE ▶ In this assignment, you are going to present your opinions in a debate on food science. As you prepare your opinions, think about the Unit Question, "How has science changed the food we eat?" Use information from Listening 1, Listening 2, and your work in this unit to support your opinions. Refer to the Self-Assessment checklist on page 124.

CONSIDER THE IDEAS

DISCUSS Work in a group. Discuss the photos below. What do you think the advantages and disadvantages of each modification are? Give reasons to support your opinion.

a. Raspberries preserved by radiation, a type of energy that can cause illness in large amounts

b. Raspberries that have not been preserved by radiation

c. A chicken that eats nonchemically treated food

d. A chicken that eats food that has been treated with artificial chemicals to make it grow much larger than normal

PREPARE AND SPEAK

A. **GATHER IDEAS** Think about the opinions you shared in the Consider the Ideas activity. Which ideas did you find most convincing? Make a short list of the three most convincing opinions on this issue.

B. **ORGANIZE IDEAS** Create a chart with two columns. Put your list of reasons from Activity A in the first column. In the second column, give details and examples to support each reason.

C. **SPEAK** Work with a partner who has different opinions on this issue. Take turns presenting your opinions and the reasons that support them. Show interest in your partner's opinions and ask questions to get more information. Refer to the Self-Assessment checklist below before you begin.

iQ PRACTICE Go online for your alternate Unit Assignment.
Practice > Unit 5 > Activity 15

CHECK AND REFLECT

A. **CHECK** Think about the Unit Assignment as you complete the Self-Assessment checklist.

SELF-ASSESSMENT	Yes	No
I was able to speak easily about the topic.	☐	☐
My partner, group, and class understood me.	☐	☐
I used comparative forms of adjectives and adverbs.	☐	☐
I used vocabulary from the unit.	☐	☐
I expressed interest during the conversation.	☐	☐
I used common intonation patterns correctly.	☐	☐
I evaluated information.	☐	☐

B. **REFLECT** Discuss these questions with a partner or group.

1. What is something new you learned in this unit?

2. Look back at the Unit Question—How has science changed the food we eat? Is your answer different now than when you started this unit? If yes, how is it different? Why?

iQ PRACTICE Go to the online discussion board to discuss the questions.
Practice > Unit 5 > Activity 16

TRACK YOUR SUCCESS

iQ PRACTICE Go online to check the words and phrases you have learned in this unit. *Practice > Unit 5 > Activity 17*

Check (✓) the skills and strategies you learned. If you need more work on a skill, refer to the page(s) in parentheses.

NOTE-TAKING	☐ I can edit my notes after a lecture. (p. 104)
LISTENING	☐ I can understand bias in a presentation. (p. 109)
CRITICAL THINKING	☐ I can evaluate information for bias. (p. 115)
VOCABULARY	☐ I can recognize and use prefixes and suffixes. (pp. 116)
GRAMMAR	☐ I can use comparative forms of adjectives and adverbs. (p. 118)
PRONUNCIATION	☐ I can use common intonation patterns. (p. 120)
SPEAKING	☐ I can express interest during a conversation. (p. 121)
OBJECTIVE ▶	☐ I can gather information and ideas to participate in a debate on food science.

SPEAKING **125**

Education 6

NOTE-TAKING	comparing and contrasting multiple topics
LISTENING	listening for contrasting ideas
CRITICAL THINKING	ranking options
VOCABULARY	using the dictionary: formal and informal words
GRAMMAR	simple, compound, and complex sentences
PRONUNCIATION	highlighted words
SPEAKING	changing the topic

UNIT QUESTION

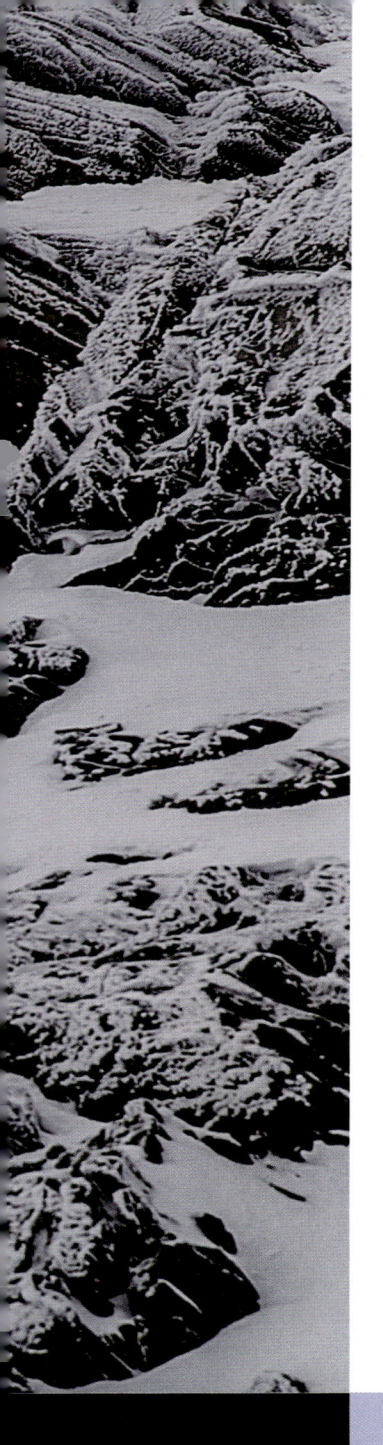

Is one road to success better than another?

A. Discuss these questions with your classmates.

1. What does being successful mean to you?
2. In your life, have you taken a traditional path or a nontraditional path to reach your educational and career goals? What are the advantages and disadvantages of each path?
3. Look at the photo. What are the people doing? How is teamwork a part of success?

B. Listen to *The Q Classroom* online. Then answer these questions.

1. Marcus thinks that different experiences give workers different perspectives. What is an example of this kind of nontraditional path to success?
2. Felix lists many steps on a traditional road to success: studying hard, getting a degree, getting work experience, getting an entry-level job, and working your way up. Which do you think is the most important step? Why?

iQ PRACTICE Go to the online discussion board to discuss the Unit Question with your classmates. *Practice > Unit 6 > Activity 1*

UNIT OBJECTIVE

Listen to two conversations, watch a video, and listen to a lecture and gather information and ideas to have a discussion and make a group decision.

NOTE-TAKING SKILL Comparing and contrasting multiple topics

When you hear information about related topics, it can be helpful to build a chart so you can easily compare and contrast the main ideas about each topic. Label the columns of your chart with the topics, and label the rows with the examples. Then write notes about each topic in the appropriate box. This is a great way to review and edit your notes after a lecture and to make connections between lectures and readings.

🔊 **A. CATEGORIZE** Listen to the class discussion about nontraditional approaches some businesses have taken to success. Complete the chart.

Company	History	Successes	Problems
Ben and Jerry's	• • • •	• •	• •
Lululemon	• • •	•	• •
Starbucks	• •	•	• •

B. SYNTHESIZE Use your notes to write a paragraph comparing and contrasting the three companies.

iQ PRACTICE Go online for more practice building a chart to compare and contrast notes on multiple topics. *Practice > Unit 6 > Activity 2*

LISTENING

LISTENING 1 Failure and Success in Startups

OBJECTIVE ▶ You are going to listen to a conversation in a business class and then watch a video. As you listen and watch, gather information and ideas about whether one road to success is better than another.

PREVIEW THE LISTENING

A. PREVIEW Before you listen, discuss the questions in a small group.

1. Do you know of anyone who has started their own small business? Were they successful? What kinds of problems have they had?

2. If you tried to start a company and it failed, what would you do? Would you try again? Would you give up? Why?

B. VOCABULARY Read aloud these words from Listening 1. Check (✓) the ones you know. Use a dictionary to define any new or unknown words. Then discuss with a partner how the words will relate to the unit.

burst (v.)	investor (n.)	profit (n.)
confidence (n.)	launch (v.)	steadily (adv.)
expand (v.) OPAL	massive (adj.)	values (n.) OPAL
genius (n.)	pressure (n.) OPAL	vision (n.)

 Oxford 5000™ words   OPAL Oxford Phrasal Academic Lexicon

iQ PRACTICE Go online to listen and practice your pronunciation.
Practice > Unit 6 > Activity 3

LISTENING 1   129

WORK WITH THE LISTENING

iQ RESOURCES Go online to watch the video.
Resources > Video > Unit 6 > Listening 1 Part 2

A. LISTEN AND TAKE NOTES Listen to the conversation. Then watch the video.* Take notes in the chart.

iQ RESOURCES Go online to download extra vocabulary support.
Resources > Extra Vocabulary > Unit 6

Businessperson	History	Problems	Successes
Scott Nash			
John Paul DeJoria (right)			
Michael Acton Smith			

B. RESTATE Work with a partner. Using your notes, take turns telling the story of each businessperson's journey to success.

* Audio version available. *Resources > Audio > Unit 6*

130   UNIT 6   Is one road to success better than another?

C. **DISCUSS** Look at your notes. Whose journey to success do you think was the easiest? Whose was the most difficult? Discuss your opinion with a partner. Use your notes to support your opinion.

D. **CATEGORIZE** Listen and watch again. Read the statements. Write *T* (true) or *F* (false). Then correct each false statement to make it true.

____ 1. Scott Nash started his business with $700.

____ 2. Scott Nash delivered food to people from his mother's house.

____ 3. MOM's Organic Market's profits are around $200,000 every year.

____ 4. John Paul DeJoria was successful as a door-to-door salesperson from the start.

____ 5. John Paul DeJoria started a hair products company alone.

____ 6. John Paul Mitchell Systems sells more than 80 products.

____ 7. Michael Acton Smith's first business plan was to sell toys, gadgets, and games on the Internet.

____ 8. Investors in Michael Acton Smith's second business lost £6,000,000.

____ 9. Michael Acton Smith believes that he would have gotten more money if Moshi Monsters had failed.

____ 10. Protecting the environment is important to all three of the businesspeople.

E. **INTERPRET** Look at the statements. Who might have made them? Write *SN* (Scott Nash), *JPD* (John Paul DeJoria), or *MAS* (Michael Acton Smith).

____ 1. "Finding investors is an important part of starting a business."

____ 2. "When you are selling something, you have to be just as excited about the product even after hundreds of doors have closed in your face."

____ 3. "Meeting the right person early on was essential for my career. I could not have been as good a salesperson without my partner's excellent product."

____ 4. "Slow growth is strong growth."

____ 5. "Don't waste a lot of your investors' money on launch events."

____ 6. "My mother supported me early in my career when I really needed the help."

LISTENING 1

F. VOCABULARY Here are some words from Listening 1. Complete each sentence with the correct word.

burst (v.)	genius (n.)	massive (adj.)	steadily (adv.)
confidence (n.)	investor (n.)	pressure (n.)	values (n.)
expand (v.)	launch (v.)	profit (n.)	vision (n.)

1. The new car will _____ in July with a big celebration.
2. He is under a lot of _____ at work. I am worried about his health.
3. He is incredibly smart. He might even be a(n) _____.
4. When he was young, he didn't believe in himself, but now he has more _____.
5. When people talk about their _____, it's easy to see what is really important to them.
6. When you climb a mountain, you don't want to move too quickly. It's better to go up slowly and _____.
7. That balloon will _____ if you add any more air to it.
8. New companies often put their _____ back into the business so it can continue to grow.
9. I believe the business will _____ into new markets under a new manager.
10. A strong leader needs to have _____ so he or she can see what the future might hold.
11. Her new business needs to look for a(n) _____. They need more money to grow.
12. The government is talking about a _____ increase in spending.

iQ PRACTICE Go online for more practice with the vocabulary.
Practice > Unit 6 > Activity 4

iQ PRACTICE Go online for additional listening and comprehension.
Practice > Unit 6 > Activity 5

SAY WHAT YOU THINK

DISCUSS Work in a group to discuss the questions.

1. The businesspeople in the conversation and video understand that failure is a necessary part of success. Why do they believe this is true? Do you agree? Why or why not?

2. Were you surprised by the challenges these people experienced? Explain.

LISTENING SKILL   Listening for contrasting ideas

When speakers **contrast** things or ideas, they use special words and phrases to point out different characteristics of the things being discussed.

The simplest way to show a contrast is to use a comparative adjective + *than*.

> He became a **better** salesperson **than** he was before.

Speakers also contrast things and ideas by using words and phrases such as *in contrast to*, *instead of*, *however*, *on the other hand*, *but*, *rather than*, and *whereas*.

> **In contrast to** Scott Nash, John Paul DeJoria wasn't a very successful salesperson at the start.
>
> So, sometimes entrepreneurs start small and steadily grow. **But** more often, starting a new business is a journey of mistakes and failures.

A. APPLY Listen to a discussion about two candidates for a job. Fill in the blanks with the contrasting words and phrases you hear.

TIP FOR SUCCESS

To understand a speaker's meaning, it's important to analyze the words and phrases they use. The way a speaker organizes and presents information is usually an important clue about what the speaker wants you to know.

Mr. Doshi: Bob Quintero and Susan Miyamoto are the final candidates for the marketing position at our company. Bob has a degree from Harvard University in the USA, _____1_____ Susan has a degree from Keio Business School in Japan.

Ms. Stanz: Bob and Susan both have good work experience. Bob has worked for five years at a small marketing company. _____2_____ Susan has worked for eight years at our company.

Mr. Doshi: Susan speaks more languages. Bob speaks Arabic and Spanish. _____3_____, Susan speaks French, Spanish, and Japanese.

Ms. Stanz: Bob has a lot of sales experience. _____4_____, Susan has a lot of experience at our company.

Mr Doshi: Hmmm. This is going to be a tough decision!

LISTENING 1   133

B. CATEGORIZE Listen to the conversation and watch the video from Listening 1 again. As you listen and watch, check (✓) the person or people each statement describes.

	Scott Nash	John Paul DeJoria	Michael Acton Smith
Started a business with a little money			
Started a business with a lot of money from investors			
Expanded his company slowly			
Learned from his early failures			
Failed because he spent too much money			
Focused on his values			
Failed two times before he succeeded			

C. COMPOSE Work with a partner. Take turns making sentences that compare Scott Nash, John Paul DeJoria, and Michael Acton Smith using words and phrases to show contrast.

| in contrast to | instead of | however | on the other hand |
| but | rather than | whereas | |

iQ PRACTICE Go online for more practice listening for contrasting ideas.
Practice > Unit 6 > Activity 6

LISTENING 2 Interns in New York

OBJECTIVE ▶ You are going to listen to a lecture and then listen to a conversation between two friends about the advantages and disadvantages of doing an internship. As you listen, gather information and ideas about whether one road to success is better than another.

PREVIEW THE LISTENING

A. PREVIEW An internship is work experience available to students and new graduates for a short period of time. The interns are sometimes not paid or paid very little. Discuss the questions in a small group.

1. Would you consider working for free in order to learn more about a job you might want to do in the future? If yes, what job would you like to try?

2. Do you know of anyone who has done an internship? What was his or her experience like?

B. VOCABULARY Read aloud these words from Listening 2. Check (✓) the ones you know. Use a dictionary to define any new or unknown words. Then discuss with a partner how the words will relate to the unit.

ACADEMIC LANGUAGE
According to the corpus, *basically* is more commonly used in academic speaking than in academic writing.

─── OPAL
Oxford Phrasal Academic Lexicon

altogether *(adv.)*	**in particular** *(idm)* OPAL
basically *(adv.)* OPAL	**meaningful** *(adj.)* OPAL
decent *(adj.)*	**miserable** *(adj.)*
disposable *(adj.)*	**predecessor** *(n.)*
fairness *(n.)*	**rate** *(n.)* OPAL
fierce *(adj.)*	**workforce** *(n.)*

Oxford 5000™ words   **OPAL** Oxford Phrasal Academic Lexicon

iQ PRACTICE Go online to listen and practice your pronunciation.
Practice > Unit 6 > Activity 7

LISTENING 2   **135**

WORK WITH THE LISTENING

A. LISTEN AND TAKE NOTES Listen to the lecture and the conversation. In the chart, list advantages and disadvantages of doing an internship.

iQ RESOURCES Go online to download extra vocabulary support.
Resources > Extra Vocabulary > Unit 6

Advantages of an internship	Disadvantages of an internship

B. EVALUATE In the Listening, HyoJin is talking with a friend, Nicholas. Do you think HyoJin's summer plans sound better than Nicholas's? Use your notes to explain your choice to a partner.

C. IDENTIFY Check (✓) the solutions to the problem of unpaid internships that are mentioned in Listening 2.

____ 1. sue the employer

____ 2. create a union to reject unpaid internships

____ 3. reduce the unemployment rate

____ 4. complain to the government

____ 5. write a letter to the management

D. IDENTIFY Read the questions. Then listen again. Circle the correct answers.

1. Why did Lucy Bickerton sue the company where she did her internship?
   a. Because she had to work too many hours every day
   b. Because she wasn't paid, even though she was doing a real job
   c. Because the company didn't hire her after she did the internship

2. What do the groups Intern Aware and the Global Intern Coalition do?
   a. Help match interns and companies
   b. Sue companies so they pay the interns
   c. Work to improve conditions for interns

3. According to the lecture, what was the unemployment rate for young people last year?

   a. 12.5%

   b. 20%

   c. 24%

4. How did HyoJin's brother benefit from his internship?

   a. He learned how to work at a big company.

   b. He was more competitive when he applied at other tech companies.

   c. He met people in the tech industry who helped him start his own company.

5. Why might HyoJin choose to take the unpaid internship?

   a. It would not be hot, dirty, or hard work.

   b. The projects will be interesting and meaningful.

   c. It will make her more competitive for other jobs.

E. RESTATE HyoJin's brother and sister had very different internship experiences. Work with a partner. Imagine and discuss what advice they might give HyoJin.

HyoJin's brother: "_____"

HyoJin's sister: "_____"

F. DISCUSS Work in a small group to discuss the questions.

1. Would internships work better in some industries than in others? What are some workplaces that would be more accommodating to interns? What are some that would not be? Why?

2. Interns are typically younger people in their early 20s. However, older workers who are changing their careers might also be interns. Are there any advantages or disadvantages to hiring an older intern? If you were a manager of a company, would you prefer to hire an older or a younger intern? Why?

3. Think of a company you might like to work at in the future. What would you be able to learn as an intern? What kinds of tasks would you do?

VOCABULARY SKILL REVIEW

In Unit 5, you learned to use prefixes and suffixes to help determine the meaning of new vocabulary words. Identify two words containing a suffix used for adverbs in Activity G.

G. VOCABULARY Here are some words from Listening 2. Read the sentences. Then write each bold word next to the correct definition.

1. When I started my new job, I changed many of the policies of my **predecessor**.
2. It is completely wrong for corporations to view workers as **disposable**.
3. I want a job that I like, but it's also important to make a **decent** salary. I need to pay rent and buy food.
4. The new leader wanted to make **meaningful** changes that would make life better for her country.
5. The pay **rate** for new employees is usually not very good.
6. He wanted to quit smoking **altogether**.
7. She has strong ideas about justice and **fairness**. She should be a judge.
8. There are more men in the **workforce** than women right now.
9. I hated my job and my boss was angry all the time. Going to work every day was a **miserable** experience.
10. The competition between the two athletes was **fierce**, and the results were very close.
11. She had some problems at her new school, but **basically,** she likes it.
12. Do you like any music **in particular**, or do you listen to all music?

a. _____ (adv.) completely
b. _____ (adj.) showing strong feelings or a lot of activity
c. _____ (adj.) of a good enough standard or quality
d. _____ (adj.) unpleasant
e. _____ (idm.) special, specific
f. _____ (n.) the people who are available for work
g. _____ (adj.) serious or important
h. _____ (adv.) in the most important ways; essentially
i. _____ (n.) a person who did a job before someone else
j. _____ (n.) treating people equally
k. _____ (adj.) that you can easily stop employing or thinking about
l. _____ (n.) an amount of money that is charged or paid for something

iQ PRACTICE Go online for more practice with the vocabulary.
Practice › Unit 6 › Activity 8

CRITICAL THINKING STRATEGY

Ranking options

Ranking helps you make decisions when you have to choose between several options. When you rank things in a group, you first need to decide which characteristics are positive and which are negative. Then you make a judgment about each option—whether it has enough advantages and not too many disadvantages. Finally, you compare each option with the other options and you put them in order, usually from what you most prefer to what you least prefer. Make sure you know why you ranked it that way.

iQ PRACTICE Go online to watch the Critical Thinking Video and check your comprehension. *Practice > Unit 6 > Activity 9*

H. EXTEND Consider the following work experience opportunities. Which opportunity would you prefer? Rank the options. Think about your choices and try to list a few reasons why you ranked them the way you did.

____ an internship at a large tech company

____ an internship at a museum

____ an internship at a small, grassroots nonprofit organization

____ an internship with a large, well-known nonprofit organization

____ working for pay in a family business

I. DISCUSS Share your list with a partner. Explain the reasons for your rankings.

SAY WHAT YOU THINK

SYNTHESIZE Think about Listening 1 and Listening 2 as you discuss the questions.

1. Would you prefer to start your own business, like the businesspeople in Listening 1, or work for an established company, like the interns in Listening 2? Why?

2. In Listening 1, the businesspeople learned from mistakes they made. In Listening 2, the interns learned from working with people who were more experienced than they were. In your opinion, which way is better? How would you prefer to learn?

VOCABULARY SKILL Using the dictionary: formal and informal words

English does not have strong rules of formality like some languages do. However, in some situations, it may be more appropriate to use certain words than others. In other more casual situations, it may be more appropriate to use less formal vocabulary, such as *phrasal verbs* and *idioms*. It is helpful to know when to use certain words and phrases.

A dictionary can guide you on which word to use. It will tell you if a word is informal or slang. If a definition doesn't say this, you can usually assume it is more formal or neutral.

Here are some examples.

> **PHR V** ˌhang aˈround (…) (*informal*) to wait or stay near a place, not doing very much: *You hang around here in case he comes, and I'll go on ahead.* ˌhang aˈround with sb (*informal*) to spend a lot of time with someone ˌhang ˈback to remain

> *those old photos—they may be valuable.* ˌhang ˈout (*informal*) to spend a lot of time in a place: *The local kids hang out at the mall.* ➔ related noun HANGOUT ˌhang ˈout with sb (*informal*)

> **so·cial·ize** /ˈsoʊʃəˌlaɪz/ *verb* **1** [I] ~ (**with sb**) to meet and spend time with people in a friendly way, in order to enjoy yourself **SYN** MIX: *I enjoy socializing with the other students.*
> • *Maybe you should socialize more.* **2** [T, often passive] ~ **sb**

The dictionary categorizes *hang around* and *hang out* as informal, but *socialize* has no description like this.

Here are some examples of appropriate use.

To your friends: I'll be <u>hanging around</u> all day.

To your family: I'm going to <u>hang out</u> with my friends today.

In a presentation: Most teenagers enjoy <u>socializing</u> with friends.

All dictionary entries adapted from the *Oxford Advanced American Dictionary for learners of English* © Oxford University Press 2011.

A. IDENTIFY Read the pairs of sentences. Check (✓) the sentence that sounds more formal.

1. ☐ a. I can always **count on** you to help me out.
   ☑ b. I always **trust** that you'll assist me.

2. ☐ a. My brother must **select** a new suit for his interview.
   ☐ b. My brother has to **pick out** a new suit for his interview.

3. ☐ a. Lately I've been **enthusiastic about** volunteering.
   ☐ b. These days I'm really **into** the idea of volunteering.

4. ☐ a. I have to **cut back** on my work hours this semester.
   ☐ b. I have to **reduce** the number of hours I work this semester.

B. IDENTIFY Read the sentences. Circle the answer that means almost the same as the bold word in each sentence.

1. I don't think we need to **hang around** here until he returns.
   a. wait   b. climb   c. joke

2. He was hoping to **get** a promotion at work.
   a. find   b. receive   c. give

3. You don't need to **put up with** a job that is so boring! Get a new one.
   a. tolerate   b. look for   c. create

4. Have you **looked into** other companies to work for? There must be many others like that one.
   a. answered   b. counted   c. researched

5. **Jumping up** a few steps at a time is almost impossible in a traditional career path.
   a. bouncing   b. advancing   c. returning

6. I've been working so hard at school. I'm **worn out**. I need to rest!
   a. prepared   b. tired   c. worried

C. APPLY Circle the appropriate synonym to complete each sentence. Then work with a partner to read the conversations.

Interviewee: Good morning. I'm here to (have a word / speak) with Ms. Lee.
                                              1

Receptionist: Please (wait / hang around) here. I'll tell Ms. Lee you're here.
                          2

Ms. Lee: Good morning. So let's (get going / begin). Can you tell me why you'd
                                      3
like to work for this company?

Interviewee: Well, I'm really (interested in / into) your products.
                                    4

iQ PRACTICE Go online for more practice using the dictionary to identify formal and informal words. *Practice > Unit 6 > Activity 10*

SPEAKING

OBJECTIVE ▶ At the end of this unit, you are going to participate in a group discussion about the qualifications of job applicants and make a hiring decision. Throughout the discussion, you will need to be able to change the topic.

GRAMMAR Simple, compound, and complex sentences

Using a variety of sentence types will allow you to express a range of ideas in your speeches and presentations.

There are three basic kinds of sentences: **simple**, **compound**, and **complex**.

A **simple sentence** is one independent clause (one subject + verb combination) that makes sense by itself.

> I want to do research.
> subject verb

A **compound sentence** is made of at least two independent clauses joined together with a conjunction, such as *and*, *but*, *or*, *yet*, and *so*.

> independent clause   independent clause
> Paul had quality hair products to sell, **and** John Paul was a good salesman.
>   conjunction

A **complex sentence** is made of at least one independent clause and one dependent clause. A dependent clause is not a complete idea by itself. The dependent clause begins with a subordinating conjunction, such as *because*, *before*, *since*, *after*, *although*, *if*, or *when*.

> independent clause   dependent clause
> I might learn a lot **if** I'm lucky and get hired by a good company.
>   subordinating conjunction

If the dependent clause comes before the independent clause, then a comma separates the two clauses.

> Although she was an unpaid intern, she was doing the work of a full-time production assistant.

iQ RESOURCES Go online to watch the Grammar Skill Video.
Resources > Video > Unit 6 > Grammar Skill Video

A. IDENTIFY Read each sentence. Is the sentence simple, compound, or complex? Circle the correct answer. Then compare answers with a partner.

1. This model is similar to the business cultures in other countries.

   (simple / compound / complex)

2. The right training is important, but what other steps do you need to take to reach your career goal?

   (simple / compound / complex)

3. Because he moved in and out of companies as positions opened, he could advance faster toward his career goal.

   (simple / compound / complex)

4. Many countries in Asia follow this business model.

   (simple / compound / complex)

5. After she worked for a year, she was ready to return to school.

   (simple / compound / complex)

B. RESTATE Rewrite the conversation below. Combine the simple sentences using the words in parentheses. Then practice the conversation.

Sam was walking down the street. He saw his friend Inez. (when)
Sam was walking down the street when he saw his friend Inez.

Inez: Hey, Sam! How did your job interview go?

Sam: Hi! It went really well. I might get the job! (and)

Inez: That's great! When will you know for sure?

Sam: They'll make the decision this afternoon. They'll call me. (after)

Inez: Good luck! By the way, did you hear about Adam?

Sam: No. I sent him an email last week. He hasn't answered it. (but)

Inez: Well, he's taking a year off. He's going to Antarctica to study penguins. (because)

Sam: Wow! That sounds amazing.

Inez: Yeah. It seems like an incredible opportunity. I can't imagine living in Antarctica. (although)

Sam: What about you? How are you going to spend the summer?

Inez: I applied to two programs. I might volunteer for a group that builds houses for people. I might work in a program for street kids. (or)

Sam: Those both sound like important projects! They'll look good on your college application. (and)

Inez: Yeah. I need to do something significant. I want to get into a good school! (if)

Sam: Well, I should get home. I can wait for the call about the job. (so)

Inez: See you later!

iQ PRACTICE Go online for more practice with simple, compound, and complex sentences. *Practice > Unit 6 > Activities 11–12*

PRONUNCIATION Highlighted words

Speakers typically use a higher pitch and longer vowel sounds to emphasize or highlight content words.

For example, a speaker might stress the words in the following sentence normally.

He <u>started</u> his <u>business</u> with <u>only one hundred dollars</u>.

Sometimes a speaker will shift the stress from this regular stress pattern to emphasize an idea. **Highlighted words** often present a contrast or a correction.

A speaker who wants to emphasize the amount of money the business started with might place a heavier stress on *one hundred*.

He <u>started</u> his <u>business</u> with <u>only **one hundred** dollars</u>.
(meaning = not two hundred dollars)

Or, if the speaker wants to correct the idea that someone else started the business, he or she might stress *he*.

He <u>started</u> his <u>business</u> with <u>only one hundred dollars</u>.
(meaning = not someone else)

Any word can be highlighted. It's important to listen for and use highlighted words carefully because they change the meaning of the sentence.

A. IDENTIFY Listen to each sentence. Underline the highlighted words you hear. Then practice saying the sentences with a partner.

1. I would love to do an internship at a major tech company.
2. If I had to pick just one place to work, it would be New York City.
3. When Carlos was there, they didn't have the internship program.
4. She's working at a new engineering company.
5. You'll learn a lot while you're there, and you'll have so much fun!

B. **INTERPRET** Listen to each sentence. What is the speaker's meaning? Circle the correct answers.

1. I would like to get a job in Zambia working with wild animals.
   a. I am interested in Zambia.
   b. I hope I have a good chance at getting the job.
   c. I'm more interested in wild animals than domestic animals.

2. I change jobs often. My father's career path was more traditional.
   a. My career path is different from my father's career path.
   b. I like to change jobs to help my career.
   c. I prefer traditional career paths.

3. I think I can build skills for this career if I take a year off to study.
   a. I'm not sure I can build my skills.
   b. I can only build skills by taking time off.
   c. If I take a year off, I have to study the whole time.

4. The best reason to do an internship is the chance to learn about yourself.
   a. This reason is very important.
   b. Learning is very important.
   c. You are very important.

5. No one ever told me that the group would leave before school is over.
   a. I expected the group to stay at the school.
   b. I thought the group would leave after school is over.
   c. They told other people, but they forgot to tell me.

C. **APPLY** Work with a partner. Practice the conversation. Stress the bold words.

A: Have you heard about Lee's **latest** plan?

B: No. What does he want to do **now**?

A: He says he **finally** decided to do an internship in a government office.

B: He wants to **do an internship**? I thought he wanted a paying job.

A: Well, it seems he changed his mind **again**.

B: Hmm. He **would** be good at it. He's a natural leader.

A: He's good at **lots** of things, so I'm sure he'll think of more ideas.

B: Yeah. He probably won't figure out where to work until **right** before he leaves!

iQ PRACTICE Go online for more practice with highlighted words.
Practice > Unit 6 > Activity 13

SPEAKING SKILL Changing the topic

In the middle of a conversation you may want to **change the topic** a little. However, you don't want to sound like you are uninterested in what someone else is saying. To let someone know you want to add something related to the topic, you can use *transition phrases*. Here are some examples:

- By the way . . .
- Speaking of (previous topic) . . .
- That reminds me . . .

For example, if your friend is talking about a book he finished reading yesterday, you can say, "Oh, speaking of books, did you hear about that new adventure novel?"

Sometimes you remember something in the middle of a conversation that is not at all related to the current topic. It is important to let others know you are about to switch to an unrelated topic. Here are some expressions you can use:

- Hold that thought.
- Oh, before I forget . . .
- Oh, I wanted to tell / ask you . . .

For example, you and two friends are talking about an exhibition. You suddenly remember you wanted to ask them about an important class project. You wait for a short pause in the conversation and then say, "Oh, before I forget, I wanted to ask you if you want to go over the project notes today."

To return to the previous topic, you can then use phrases like these:

- But you were saying . . .
- Back to (the topic) . . .
- Anyway . . .

A. APPLY Complete the conversation with the words you hear. Then practice the conversation with a partner.

A: I've had a very long day. I just came from my job.

B: _____ 1, I need to get your résumé. My company is hiring, and you would be perfect for the position.

A: Really? That's great! You make your job sound fun.

B: It is, most of the time. We all get along well at work.

A: Oh, _____ 2 if you have time to help me with my homework.

B: Sure I can. We'll do it after class.

A: _____, I'd love to give you my résumé. I've been looking for a new job.

B: I know. _____, my boss says she's interviewing people next week. Are you free in the morning?

A: I'll make sure I'm available if she calls me.

B: _____. I have to get to my next class. We'll talk about this later.

A: See you.

B. EXTEND Work in a group. Discuss the questions. Practice changing and returning to topics.

1. What does it mean to be successful? How do you define it for yourself?
2. What are the characteristics of a dream job? What steps should someone take—traditional and nontraditional—to get their dream job?
3. What type of person is most likely to achieve his or her dream job?

iQ PRACTICE Go online for more practice changing the topic.
Practice > Unit 6 > Activity 14

UNIT ASSIGNMENT Reach a group decision
OBJECTIVE ▶

In this assignment, you are going to have a discussion in order to reach a group decision. As you prepare for your discussion, think about the Unit Question, "Is one road to success better than another?" Use information from Listening 1, Listening 2, and your work in this unit to support your discussion. Refer to the Self-Assessment checklist on page 150.

CONSIDER THE IDEAS

Complete the activities.

1. Read the following advertisement for a job opening.

GAPSTAFF NEEDS YOU!

GapStaff is looking for a consultant to join our exciting and energetic team. Consultants are responsible for working with clients to organize their gap year opportunities. Candidates for the job should be well organized, interesting in working with students, and passionate about traveling, learning, and volunteering.

The minimum requirements for the position are an undergraduate degree and five years of related work experience.
Travel experience and the ability to speak another language are a plus.

2. Read the information about four people who applied for the GapStaff consultant job. Then listen to their personal statements. Take notes in the chart.

Personal information	Notes

Susan Jones (age 59)
Education:
  A.A. in Journalism from Central Texas College
  B.A. in English from the University of Chicago
Work Experience:
  English teacher in Poland (3 years)
  English teacher in Morocco (2 years)
  English teacher in Peru (6 years)	

Doug Orman (age 43)
Education:
  B.A. in History from the University of Maryland
  M.A. in History from the University of Maryland
Work Experience:
  Teaching Assistant at the University of Maryland (3 years)
  Lecturer at the University of Maryland (16 years)	

148 UNIT 6 Is one road to success better than another?

Personal information	Notes

Narayan Tej (age 24)
Education:
  B.A. in Tourism from Columbia Southern University
Work Experience:
  Part-time work at the tourism desk of the Hilton Hotel	

Teresa Lopez (age 35)
Education:
  B.S. in Business Administration from National American University
Work Experience:
  Guide at local museum (3 years)
  Receptionist for travel agent (2 years)
  Receptionist for gym (5 years)
  Salesperson at clothing store (2 years)	

PREPARE AND SPEAK

A. GATHER IDEAS Imagine you are part of a GapStaff group choosing the best candidate for the position. Consider the four job applicants. Who do you think is most qualified? Who is least qualified? Rank the applicants from 1 (your first choice) to 4 (your last choice), based on your notes in the chart above.

____ Susan Jones   ____ Narayan Tej

____ Doug Orman   ____ Teresa Lopez

B. ORGANIZE IDEAS Why did you rank the candidates in this order? Complete the chart with brief notes.

Candidate name	Reasons for ranking
1.	
2.	
3.	
4.	

C. SPEAK Work in a group. Discuss who should be hired for the position. Share your reasons with the group. Work to reach a group decision on the best person to hire. Refer to the Self-Assessment checklist below before you begin.

iQ PRACTICE Go online for your alternate Unit Assignment.
Practice > Unit 6 > Activity 15

CHECK AND REFLECT

A. CHECK Think about the Unit Assignment as you complete the Self-Assessment checklist.

SELF-ASSESSMENT	Yes	No
I was able to speak easily about the topic.	☐	☐
My partner, group, and class understood me.	☐	☐
I listened for contrasting ideas.	☐	☐
I used vocabulary from the unit.	☐	☐
I changed the topic in the discussion.	☐	☐
I highlighted words to emphasize ideas as I spoke.	☐	☐
I ranked options.	☐	☐

B. REFLECT Discuss these questions with a partner or group.

1. What is something new you learned in this unit?
2. Look back at the Unit Question—Is one road to success better than another? Is your answer different now than when you started this unit? If yes, how is it different? Why?

iQ PRACTICE Go to the online discussion board to discuss the questions.
Practice > Unit 6 > Activity 16

TRACK YOUR SUCCESS

iQ PRACTICE Go online to check the words and phrases you have learned in this unit. *Practice > Unit 6 > Activity 17*

Check (✓) the skills and strategies you learned. If you need more work on a skill, refer to the page(s) in parentheses.

NOTE-TAKING	☐ I can compare and contrast multiple topics. (p. 128)
LISTENING	☐ I can listen for contrasting ideas. (p. 133)
CRITICAL THINKING	☐ I can rank options based on advantages and disadvantages. (p. 139)
VOCABULARY	☐ I can use the dictionary to find formal or informal words. (p. 140)
GRAMMAR	☐ I can use simple, compound, and complex sentences. (p. 142)
PRONUNCIATION	☐ I can highlight words to emphasize ideas. (p. 144)
SPEAKING	☐ I can change the topic. (p. 146)
OBJECTIVE ▶	☐ I can gather information and ideas to have a discussion in order to reach a group decision.

7 Anthropology

LISTENING	listening for signal words and phrases
NOTE-TAKING	taking notes on details
VOCABULARY	collocations with prepositions
GRAMMAR	indirect speech
PRONUNCIATION	linked words with vowels
SPEAKING	using questions to maintain listener interest
CRITICAL THINKING	combining ideas

UNIT QUESTION

How can accidental discoveries affect our lives?

A. Discuss these questions with your classmates.

1. The journalist Franklin Adams once wrote, "I find that a great part of the information I have was acquired by looking up something and finding something else on the way." What do you think he meant?

2. Have you ever discovered something important by accident? If so, what was it? How did the discovery affect you?

3. Look at the photo. Why might this place be a good space for an accidental discovery? What might you discover in a place like this?

B. Listen to *The Q Classroom* online. Then answer these questions.

1. Marcus says that it is important to keep learning and having new experiences. Do you agree with him? What does his advice have to do with making accidental discoveries?

2. Each student talks about accidental discoveries in a very positive way. Do you think there are some situations where accidental discoveries aren't so positive? If so, in what situations?

iQ PRACTICE Go to the online discussion board to discuss the Unit Question with your classmates. *Practice > Unit 7 > Activity 1*

UNIT OBJECTIVE ▶ Listen to two reports and gather information and ideas to tell a personal story about an accidental discovery you made and how it affected you.

153

LISTENING

LISTENING 1   The Power of Serendipity

OBJECTIVE ▶ You are going to listen to a news report about how accidental discoveries have led to some important scientific developments. As you listen to the report, gather information and ideas about how accidental discoveries can affect our lives.

PREVIEW THE LISTENING

A. PREVIEW Scientists work hard to keep control of their work and make sure mistakes do not happen. How often do you think accidents play a role in scientific discoveries? Discuss with a partner.

B. VOCABULARY Read aloud these words from Listening 1. Check (✓) the ones you know. Use a dictionary to define any new or unknown words. Then discuss with a partner how the words will relate to the unit.

adhesive (n.)	inconceivable (adj.)	synthetic (adj.)
exploit (v.) OPAL	interact (v.) OPAL	unreliable (adj.)
flammable (adj.)	mandatory (adj.)	vastly (adv.)
inadvertent (adj.)	obvious (adj.) OPAL	

 Oxford 5000™ words   OPAL Oxford Phrasal Academic Lexicon

iQ PRACTICE Go online to listen and practice your pronunciation.
Practice > Unit 7 > Activity 2

WORK WITH THE LISTENING

A. LISTEN AND TAKE NOTES Take notes about the main ideas and important details you hear.

Main ideas	Important details

B. CREATE Review your notes from Activity A and write questions. These can be questions your teacher might ask, questions answered in the listening, or other questions you would like to find answers to. Then compare your notes and questions with a partner.

C. IDENTIFY Use your notes to match each scientific breakthrough with the accident or event that led to it. Then listen again to check your answers.

Accident or Event

____ 1. Alfred Nobel worked with a flammable medicine.

____ 2. A sticky substance was mixed with sulfur and dropped on a hot stove.

____ 3. An Ethiopian goat herder watched his goats eating.

____ 4. Nomads traveled on camels carrying milk in stomach bags.

____ 5. A scientist tried to invent a new form of adhesive, but it was very weak.

____ 6. Scientists tried to create synthetic rubber but failed.

Scientific Breakthrough

a. The effects of coffee beans were discovered.

b. Rubber became a useful product.

c. Cheese was made for the first time.

d. Dynamite was discovered.

e. Silly Putty® was invented.

f. Post-it Notes® were invented.

D. CATEGORIZE Read the statements. Write *T* (true) or *F* (false). Then correct each false statement to make it true.

___ 1. Serendipity is looking for one thing and finding something more valuable by accident.

___ 2. Food serendipity has little to do with animals.

___ 3. Serendipity rarely plays a role in products we purchase today.

___ 4. Serendipity is a source of innovation.

___ 5. According to one of the speakers, serendipity is a luxury that is nice but not necessary.

E. EXTEND Which items do you think were discovered or invented by accident? Compare your choices with a partner. Then conduct some research to find out if your choices are correct.

1. chocolate chip cookies
2. rechargeable batteries
3. tea
4. the pacemaker
5. Velcro®
6. Global Positioning System (GPS)

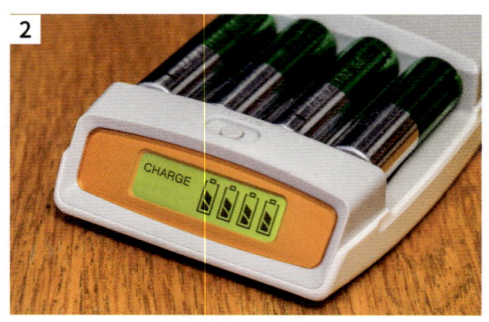

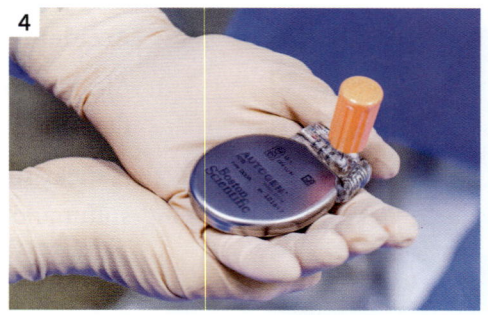

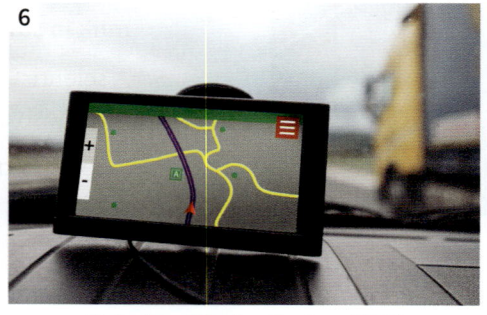

F. VOCABULARY Here are some words from Listening 1. Read the sentences. Circle the answer that best matches the meaning of each bold word.

1. Please keep **flammable** objects away from the stove. It isn't safe while we're cooking.
   a. easily breaks
   b. easily burns

2. My car is **unreliable**. I often take the bus to work because my car won't start.
   a. cannot be depended on
   b. cannot be understood

3. Miteb made an **inadvertent** discovery as he drove to the airport. He took the wrong exit, turned left, and was at the airport. Now he knows a faster route!
   a. not done on purpose
   b. not important to remember

4. Solar energy is a great source of power but not enough people use it. We must learn to **exploit** it more fully.
   a. to use something for benefit
   b. to save something

5. There is an **obvious** connection between getting overtired and getting sick.
   a. hard to understand
   b. easy to see

6. We need a strong **adhesive** to hang the poster on the wall. Otherwise, the poster will just fall off.
   a. glue
   b. surface

7. Not long ago, there was no wireless communication. But now, living without it is **inconceivable** for many people.
   a. hard to find
   b. hard to imagine

8. Nawaf and I have **vastly** different taste in clothes.
   a. hardly
   b. very greatly

9. Many people like to use websites to **interact** with people that have similar interests.
   a. get contact information
   b. communicate

10. Attendance at our monthly meetings is **mandatory**. Everyone must attend.
    a. exciting
    b. required

11. According to my auto mechanic, **synthetic** oil is better for my car than regular oil. He says man-made oil lasts longer.
    a. not natural
    b. not expensive

iQ PRACTICE Go online for more practice with the vocabulary.
Practice > Unit 7 > Activity 3

iQ PRACTICE Go online for additional listening and comprehension.
Practice > Unit 7 > Activity 4

SAY WHAT YOU THINK

DISCUSS Work in a group to discuss the questions.

1. Several of the products mentioned in the report were invented by scientists who were working hard to invent something else. What do you think this tells us about serendipity?

2. Some of the research and experiments mentioned in the report are paid for by businesses. Do you think this is a wise investment for the businesses? Why or why not?

3. One speaker in the report says serendipity is mandatory. Do you agree with this? Give reasons to support your answer.

LISTENING SKILL Listening for signal words and phrases

When you are listening to a speaker and hear a word you don't recognize, continue listening for a definition. Sometimes, speakers will give the meaning of a word they just used. Good speakers use **signal words and phrases** to clarify what they mean. Here are some examples.

This refers to . . .	What I mean by ____ is . . .
This means . . .	What is ____? It's . . .
A(n) ____ is . . .	____, or ____, . . .

Sometimes speakers say the same idea in a different way to make the meaning clear. Here are some ways that speakers signal they are about to provide an explanation.

| What I mean is . . . | Here's what this means . . . |
| In other words . . . | In simpler terms, this means . . . |

Listening for signals like these will help you to understand important words and concepts that speakers introduce.

A. APPLY Read and listen to the lecture. Fill in the blanks with the signal words and phrases you hear.

Professor: Many people use a microwave oven every day. How many of you know that the microwave oven was the result of an accident?

During World War II, scientists invented the magnetron, _____1 a kind of electronic tube that produces microwaves. We're all familiar with microwave ovens, but _____2 a microwave? Well, it's a very short electromagnetic wave.

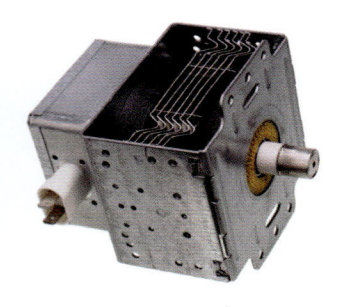

a magnetron

158   UNIT 7   How can accidental discoveries affect our lives?

Anyway, in 1946, an engineer named Dr. Percy Spencer was standing close to a magnetron he was testing. He suddenly noticed something unusual. He felt something warm in his shirt pocket. He reached in and discovered that the candy bar in his pocket was a hot, chocolaty mess. _____₃, the candy bar had melted. Dr. Spencer was so excited because he realized that microwaves could raise the internal temperature of food. _____₄, microwaves were able to cook food from the inside out! And do it very quickly.

Dr. Spencer saw the possibilities here. His next step was to build a metal box into which he fed microwave power that couldn't escape. He put various foods inside the metal box and tested cooking them. In time, he invented something that would revolutionize cooking—the ubiquitous microwave oven. By that _____₅ that we see microwave ovens just about everywhere.

B. IDENTIFY Read the sentences. Complete each sentence with a signal word or phrase from the Listening Skill box. Then practice reading the sentences with a partner.

1. It was all by accident. _____
   the invention was the result of serendipity.

2. There were endless possibilities. _____
   _____ the new discovery could be used for many different things.

3. Then a light bulb went off. _____
   I realized what I had to do to make it work correctly.

4. It was a stupendous success. _____
   _____ it worked better than anyone had hoped.

5. Soon it will be commonplace. _____
   _____ everyone will own one and love it!

"A light bulb went off."

iQ PRACTICE Go online for more practice listening for signal words and phrases. *Practice > Unit 7 > Activity 5*

LISTENING 1 159

NOTE-TAKING SKILL Taking notes on details

When you take notes on a report or a story, write down details that are important to the account. Try to list specific names and dates, along with major events and their effects. Do not try to write complete sentences. Instead, just write down key words and phrases to help you remember the details. When you review your notes, the list of details will provide you with a kind of timeline and will help you recall the major people, events, and facts.

A. IDENTIFY Listen and read the account of a major archaeological discovery. Take notes on the important details that make up the story.

A Walk to Remember

The year was 1940, and Marcel Ravidat was a French 18-year-old. One day he did what he often liked to do. He went for a walk in the woods near his home. He was with two friends and his dog, Robot. They had strolled along those same trails many times, but this day would be different. Marcel would stumble upon something amazing.

Actually, you could say that Robot literally stumbled upon it. Some say that as the group was walking through the woods, the little dog ran off. Marcel and his friends ran after it, trying to keep up. When they finally caught up to Robot, they found him digging down into a hole that had been left by a collapsed tree. And for some reason Marcel began to help Robot dig. He didn't realize that he was about to make a huge archaeological discovery.

The hole he was digging turned out to lead to a system of caves. Marcel climbed down into the cave through the widened hole, and there he found a series of prehistoric wall paintings. There were many of them, and they depicted animals—bulls, horses, and deer—in bright colors.

The discovery became a major news event. Researchers were amazed by it, and tourists flocked to the site from around the world. In fact, so many people visited the cave that in 1963 it had to be closed off again to protect the paintings.

Marcel's discovery was as historic as it was unexpected. When he headed out into those familiar woods that morning, he had no idea that he would find a passageway to another time, to another world.

B. CATEGORIZE Compare your notes with a partner. Did you miss any important details? Did you list any details that you now think are unnecessary? Use your notes to make a timeline of the main events in the story.

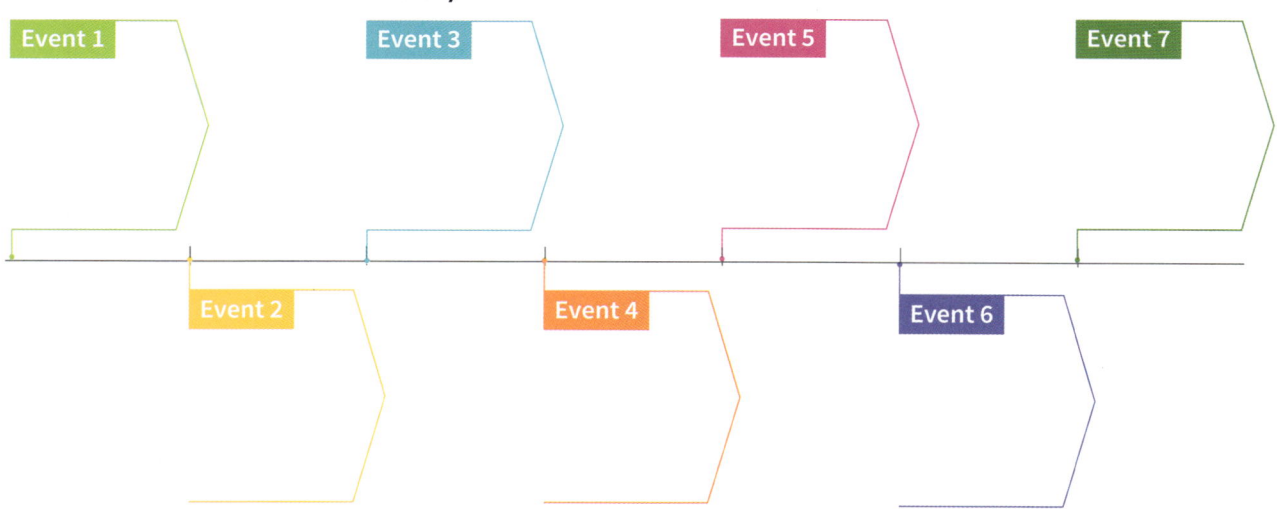

Event 1 | Event 2 | Event 3 | Event 4 | Event 5 | Event 6 | Event 7

iQ PRACTICE Go online for more practice taking notes on details.
Practice > Unit 7 > Activity 6

LISTENING 2 Against All Odds, Twin Girls Reunited

OBJECTIVE ▶ You are going to listen to a report about how twins were reunited unexpectedly. As you listen to the report, gather information and ideas about how accidental discoveries can affect our lives.

PREVIEW THE LISTENING

A. PREVIEW If two siblings were separated as babies and then met many years later, do you think they would still feel an emotional connection? Check (✓) *yes* or *no*. Discuss your answer with a partner.

☐ yes ☐ no

B. VOCABULARY Read aloud these words from Listening 2. Check (✓) the ones you know. Use a dictionary to define any new or unknown words. Then discuss with a partner how the words will relate to the unit.

ache (v.)	biological (adj.)	in all probability (adv. phr.)
adopt (v.) OPAL	deprived (adj.)	odds (n.)
alert (adj.)	face to face (adv. phr.)	reunion (n.)

 Oxford 5000™ words   OPAL Oxford Phrasal Academic Lexicon

iQ PRACTICE Go online to listen and practice your pronunciation.
Practice > Unit 7 > Activity 7

WORK WITH THE LISTENING

🔊 **A. LISTEN AND TAKE NOTES** List the important details you hear in the report. Do not try to write complete sentences. Instead, write down only the important words.

B. CATEGORIZE Use your notes to complete the timeline. Choose the events you think are most important. Then compare your answers with a partner.

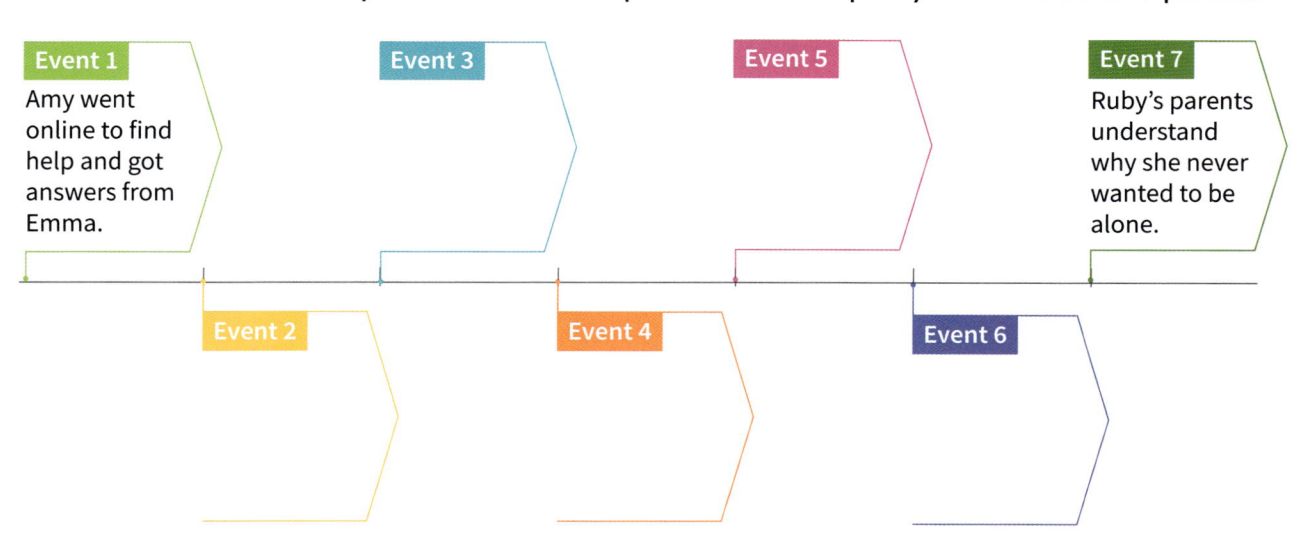

Event 1 Amy went online to find help and got answers from Emma.

Event 2

Event 3

Event 4

Event 5

Event 6

Event 7 Ruby's parents understand why she never wanted to be alone.

🔊 **C. EXPLAIN** Listen again. Then answer the questions.

1. How did Emma Smith and Amy White first get to know each other?

2. Why was Kate's mother, Amy, shocked when she saw the photograph of Ruby?

3. How did Ruby and Kate get along when they saw each other for the second time at a reunion?

4. Why did the parents decide to have a DNA test performed?

LISTENING 2 **163**

5. What did the DNA test results show?
   _____
   _____

6. How did Ruby react to the test results?
   _____
   _____

D. IDENTIFY Read the questions. Circle the correct answers.

1. Where were Ruby and Kate born?
   a. They were born in Florida.
   b. They were born in China.

2. How did Ruby behave when she first went to live with her adoptive parents?
   a. She cried a lot.
   b. She slept a lot.

3. How did Kate behave when she went to live with her new parents?
   a. She ate a lot.
   b. She cried a lot.

4. What advice did Emma Smith give Amy about dealing with Kate's eating problem?
   a. She suggested that they share a plate in the middle of the table.
   b. She suggested that they let Kate eat as much as she wanted.

5. Why did Emma and Amy exchange photographs of their daughters?
   a. They noticed that their daughters shared the same date of birth.
   b. They noticed that their daughters were from the same orphanage.

6. What reason does Kate give for why she and Ruby would like to live next door to each other?
   a. They want to go to the same school.
   b. They want to play together.

7. According to Emma Smith, why did Ruby never want to be alone?
   a. She was scared of her new parents.
   b. She had never been alone, even before she was born.

E. DISCUSS Work in a group to discuss the questions.

1. Do you think it is a good idea to encourage the relationship between the two sisters? If so, do you think these families are doing enough to help the sisters?

2. According to the mothers, the girls seemed to "remember" each other and have a natural bond. How would you explain the girls' immediate relationship?

F. VOCABULARY Here are some words from Listening 2. Complete each sentence with the correct word.

VOCABULARY SKILL REVIEW

In Unit 4, you learned that in some cases, different parts of speech of a word have the same form. For example, *ache* is spelled the same when it is used as a noun and as a verb. Find two other vocabulary words from Activity F that stay the same in different parts of speech.

ache (v.)	biological (adj.)	in all probability (adv. phr.)
adopt (v.)	deprived (adj.)	odds (n.)
alert (adj.)	face to face (adv. phr.)	reunion (n.)

1. Amy and Ed have one son. Next year they want to _____ another baby boy. Then they will have two sons.

2. I'm looking forward to our class _____. I haven't seen my classmates in so many years!

3. Derek is usually late to class. _____, he'll be late today as well.

4. My brother may be adopted, but I feel like he's my _____ brother.

5. Ever since Lisa was a baby, she has been very _____. She seems to notice everything that happens around her.

6. Eric was in a serious car accident, but the _____ that he will recover completely are very good.

7. I think I'm getting old. Every morning my knees _____, and my back hurts, too.

8. Although we have texted and emailed each other many times, Janet and I have never met _____. I hope I get to meet her someday.

9. Lucas was born in a very poor city and was _____ of many things. He rarely had a home to sleep in.

iQ PRACTICE Go online for more practice with the vocabulary.
Practice › Unit 7 › Activity 8

WORK WITH THE VIDEO

A. PREVIEW What have scientists learned about how the human brain functions?

VIDEO VOCABULARY

rod *(n.)* a long straight piece of wood, metal, or glass

puncture *(v.)* to make a small hole in something

vulgar *(adj.)* rude and likely to offend

controversial *(adj.)* causing a lot of angry public discussion and disagreement

homogeneous *(adj.)* consisting of things or people that are all the same or all of the same type

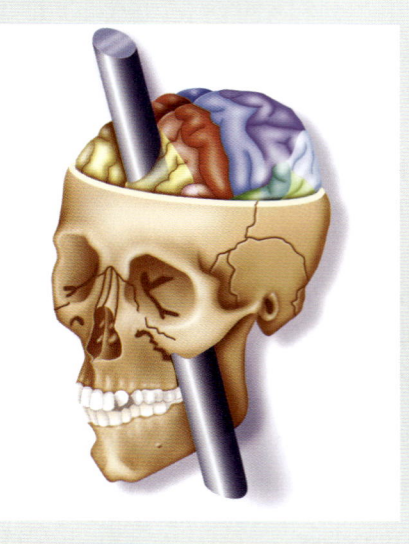

Phineas Gage

iQ RESOURCES Go online to watch the video about how the tragedy of Phineas Gage helped us discover more about the human brain.
Resources > Video > Unit 7 > Unit Video

B. CATEGORIZE Watch the video two or three times. Take notes about the details you hear. Use your notes to make a timeline of the main events in the story.

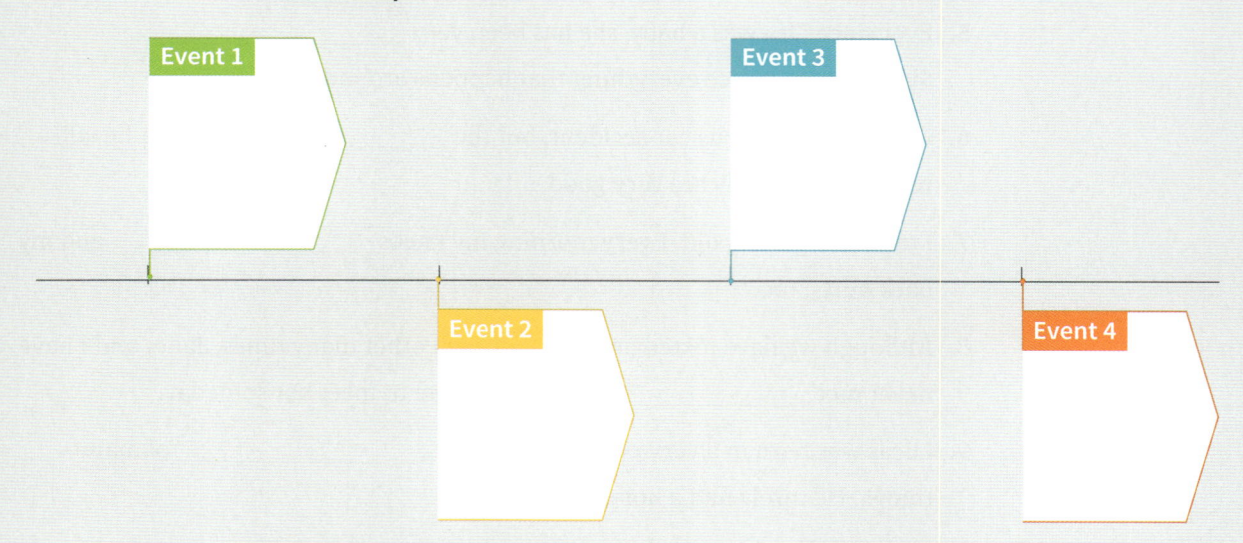

Event 1

Event 2

Event 3

Event 4

C. EXTEND What might be the disadvantages to relying on serendipity to help us understand the human brain?

166   UNIT 7   How can accidental discoveries affect our lives?

SAY WHAT YOU THINK

SYNTHESIZE Think about Listening 1, Listening 2, and the unit video as you discuss the questions.

1. Think about the scientific discoveries discussed in the unit video and Listening 1 and the personal discovery from Listening 2. Do you think all of these discoveries were truly accidental? What factors may have helped lead people to these discoveries?

2. Can you think of any ways in which accidental discoveries may have a negative effect on our lives? Discuss any examples you can think of. Consider both scientific discoveries and personal discoveries.

VOCABULARY SKILL Collocations with prepositions

Collocations are combinations of words that are used together frequently. For example, some adjectives and verbs are commonly used with particular prepositions. Part of learning to use these adjectives and verbs correctly involves knowing which prepositions are often used with them.

Here are a few **adjective + preposition** collocations.

| embarrassed about | happy about | ready for |
| fond of | proud of | upset about |

Here are a few **verb + preposition** collocations.

| complain about | believe in | decide on |
| arrive at | trip over | approve of |

Some collocations are *separable*. A direct object can come between the verb and the preposition.

bring the twins **together**   **combine** the rubber **with** sulfur

Using common collocations will help you develop your fluency.

A. IDENTIFY Listen to these sentences. Circle the prepositions that you hear.

TIP FOR SUCCESS

Look up verbs and adjectives in a collocations dictionary to find out which prepositions they are commonly used with. It's useful to learn these phrases as you would learn single words.

1. She was looking around, and she was very aware ____ what was going on.
    a. for   b. over   c. of

2. Since it's important ____ Kate, I think it's important to all of us.
    a. at   b. for   c. to

3. Because we hardly ever fight, and we agree ____ a lot of things.
    a. about   b. on   c. in

4. My daughter has not asked me a single question about her birth family or searching ____ them since she's got Kate in her life.
    a. with   b. about   c. for

LISTENING 2   167

B. APPLY Read the sentences. Complete each sentence with a collocation from the box.

| afraid of | stumbling over |
| filled ____ with | mixed ____ with |

1. The idea is to have them interact in open play-like environments, to encourage them not to be _____ failure, and to build together.

2. Serendipity refers to looking for one thing and _____ something else.

3. Rubber was an unreliable, smelly mess until Charles Goodyear _____ it _____ sulfur.

4. Nomads _____ bags _____ milk and hung them from their saddles as they rode camels.

iQ PRACTICE Go online for more practice using collocations with prepositions.
Practice > Unit 7 > Activity 9

SPEAKING

OBJECTIVE ▶ At the end of this unit, you are going to tell a personal story about an accidental discovery you made and how it affected you. As you tell the story, you will need to use questions to maintain listener interest.

GRAMMAR Indirect speech

Direct speech reports what someone said using the speaker's exact words.

- The teacher said, "You will have a test on Friday."

Indirect speech also reports what someone said, but without using the speaker's exact words.

- The teacher said we would have a test on Friday.

When using indirect speech to report what a speaker said in the past, the verb the speaker used must be changed to a past form.

> **Direct speech:**
> Wells said, "The whole idea **is** to bring together people with vastly different backgrounds."
>
> **Indirect speech:**
> Wells said the whole idea **was** to bring together people with vastly different backgrounds.

When using indirect speech to report a *yes/no* question, use *if* or *whether*.

> **Direct speech:**
> Kate asked her mother, "Is Ruby from China?"
>
> **Indirect speech:**
> Kate asked her mother **if** Ruby was from China.

When using indirect speech to report a *wh-* question, use the same *wh-* word as the speaker.

> **Direct speech:**
> He asked the professor, "**When** was the microwave oven developed?"
>
> **Indirect speech:**
> He asked the professor **when** the microwave oven was developed.

When using indirect speech to report information that is generally true or still true now, it is not necessary to shift the verb to a past form.

> **Direct speech:**
> Kate said, "**It's** fun being with Ruby."
>
> **Indirect speech:**
> Kate said that **it's** fun being with Ruby.

iQ RESOURCES Go online to watch the Grammar Skill Video.
Resources > Video > Unit 7 > Grammar Skill Video

A. CATEGORIZE Listen to each sentence. Is it direct or indirect speech? Circle the correct answers.

1. direct   indirect   5. direct   indirect
2. direct   indirect   6. direct   indirect
3. direct   indirect   7. direct   indirect
4. direct   indirect   8. direct   indirect

B. RESTATE Read these sentences. Rewrite each sentence, changing the direct speech to indirect speech. Then work with a partner to practice saying both versions of each sentence.

1. The professor said, "The discovery of dynamite is an example of serendipity."
   _____

2. Mary Tanner said, "My favorite accidental discovery is the invention of Post-it Notes."
   _____

3. The professor said, "Dr. Spencer invented something that would revolutionize cooking."
   _____

4. The professor said, "We see microwave ovens just about everywhere."
   _____

5. Amy said, "I was shocked."
   _____

6. Ruby said, "The hole in my heart is getting smaller."
   _____

7. Ruby said, "I am Kate," and Kate said, "I am Ruby."
   _____

8. In her message, Emma said, "I don't know if my baby knows Amy's baby."
   _____

iQ PRACTICE Go online for more practice with indirect speech. *Practice › Unit 7 › Activity 10*

iQ PRACTICE Go online for the Grammar Expansion: punctuation in direct and indirect speech. *Practice › Unit 7 › Activity 11*

PRONUNCIATION Linked words with vowels

Speakers often link words together so that the last sound in one word connects to the first sound in the next word. Sometimes it's difficult to tell where one word ends and another word begins.

When words ending with the vowel sounds -ee, -ey, -ay, and -oy are followed by a word beginning with a vowel, the vowels in the two words link together with the /y/ sound. Because the words are pronounced with no pause between them, it may sound like the second word begins with /y/.

Listen to these sentences and notice how the bold words link with a /y/ sound.

She **always** wants to **say it**.

Tell me **why it's** important to **be early**.

When words ending with the vowel sounds -oo, and -oh are followed by a word beginning with a vowel, the vowels link together with the /w/ sound. Because the words are pronounced with no pause between them, it may sound like the second word begins with /w/.

Listen to these sentences and notice how the bold words link with a /w/ sound.

Can she **go out** with us?

Please **show us** your **new invention**.

Linking words is an important part of fluent pronunciation. Practicing this skill will help to make your speech sound more natural.

A. APPLY Listen to these pairs of words. Then repeat the words.

1. early age
2. very alert
3. stay awake
4. fly out
5. you opened
6. know about
7. go over
8. how interesting

B. APPLY Listen to these sentences. Draw a line to show where the vowels link together. Write *y* or *w* between the words to show the linking sound. Then practice saying the sentences with a partner.

1. Kate also seemed very deprived, because they noticed she ʸate as if she'd never eat again.
2. After the fact, serendipity always seems so obvious.
3. Because we hardly ever fight, we agree on a lot of things.
4. Try and spot the next big thing.
5. So after you opened the file, can you recall how it felt?

iQ PRACTICE Go online for more practice with linked words with vowels.
Practice > Unit 7 > Activity 12

SPEAKING SKILL Using questions to maintain listener interest

When giving a presentation or telling a story, you can keep listeners interested by asking them questions. At the beginning of a presentation, a question can spark interest in your topic. During a presentation, a question can help maintain interest. At the end of your presentation, a question encourages your listeners to keep thinking about your topic after you are done speaking.

There are two main types of questions that speakers ask an audience.

Rhetorical questions are questions that do not require an answer from the audience. Use them to get your listeners to think about what you are about to say.

> What was the most important invention of the twentieth century?
> We all might not agree, but today I'd like to talk to you about one very important invention . . .

Interactive questions are questions for which you expect an answer. Use them to interact with your listeners and encourage them to respond to what you are saying.

> **Presenter:** Does anyone know who discovered the law of gravity?
> **Audience member:** I think it was Isaac Newton.
> **Presenter:** That's right. And the story behind that discovery is an interesting one . . .

Using questions when you present is an effective way to keep the audience paying attention and to help them remember your most important points.

A. EVALUATE Listen to the excerpts from lectures. Which questions are rhetorical and which are interactive? Circle the correct answers.

1. rhetorical   interactive   3. rhetorical   interactive
2. rhetorical   interactive   4. rhetorical   interactive

B. IDENTIFY Listen to this short story about another accidental invention. Then answer the questions.

The Popsicle™

The Popsicle™ is a popular summertime treat in the United States. Kids have been enjoying them for decades. But most people don't know that the Popsicle™ was invented by an 11-year-old.

In 1905, Frank Epperson filled a cup with water and fruit-flavored "soda powder," a mix that was used to make a popular drink. Frank left his drink outside on his porch with a stir stick in it. He forgot all about it and went to bed. That night, the temperature dropped to below freezing in San Francisco, where Frank lived. When he woke up the next morning, he discovered that his fruit drink had frozen to the stir stick. He pulled the frozen mixture out of the cup by the stick, creating a fruit-flavored ice treat.

In 1923, Frank Epperson began making and selling his ice treats in different flavors. By 1928, Frank had sold over 60 million Popsicles™, and his business had made him very wealthy. Nowadays, over three million Popsicles™ are sold each year.

Popsicles™ aren't the only invention made by accident. But they might be the tastiest.

TIP FOR SUCCESS
When asking interactive questions, make sure to give your listeners enough time to answer.

1. Which of these would be the most appropriate rhetorical question to start a presentation about this story?
   a. What is one of the tastiest treats ever invented?
   b. What year did Frank Epperson sell his first Popsicle™?
   c. What is the number of Popsicles™ sold every year?

2. Which of these would be the most appropriate interactive question to ask about how Frank Epperson discovered his frozen treat?
   a. What was Frank's favorite flavor of soda water?
   b. What city did Frank live in?
   c. What do you think Frank found the next morning when he went outside?

3. Which of these would be the most appropriate question to ask at the conclusion of your presentation?
   a. Why did Frank choose the name Popsicle™?
   b. Doesn't a Popsicle™ sound tasty right now?
   c. Which is the most popular flavor?

C. RESTATE In a group, practice telling the story in Activity B in your own words. Use questions to keep your listeners' interest.

iQ PRACTICE Go online for more practice using questions to maintain listener interest. *Practice › Unit 7 › Activity 13*

CRITICAL THINKING STRATEGY

Combining ideas

Putting ideas together in a new way shows you understand material and can think creatively. For instance, on many standardized English exams, you have to combine the ideas in a listening text and a reading text and show how they are connected. Also, when you combine the ideas from your textbook with the ideas shared in a lecture, you will have a deeper understanding of the course materials.

iQ PRACTICE Go online to watch the Critical Thinking Video and check your comprehension. *Practice › Unit 7 › Activity 14*

D. SYNTHESIZE Work with a partner. Read the paragraphs and brainstorm about how the Rosetta Stone and emojis might have the same function. Take notes about how the Rosetta Stone and emojis are similar. Share your ideas with a partner.

The Rosetta Stone	Emojis
In July 1799, two French soldiers discovered a piece of stone with symbols all over it. It eventually helped Egyptologists understand Ancient Egyptian hieroglyphs because it had the same text written in three different ways: hieroglyphics, ancient Greek, and another Ancient Egyptian script.	Emojis are everywhere. Some studies show they are used by up to 90% of the population. Emojis, as I am sure you know, are a pictographic and ideographic writing system that uses symbols to represent an object or idea without using words.

174 UNIT 7 How can accidental discoveries affect our lives?

UNIT ASSIGNMENT Tell a story

OBJECTIVE ▶

In this assignment, you are going to tell a personal story about an accidental discovery you made and how it affected you. As you prepare your story, think about the Unit Question, "How can accidental discoveries affect our lives?" Use information from Listening 1, Listening 2, the unit video, and your work in this unit to support your story. Refer to the Self-Assessment checklist on page 176.

CONSIDER THE IDEAS

Look at the list of ideas about discovery. Choose the four ideas you think are the most important factors in making any kind of discovery. Then discuss your answers and reasons with a partner.

desire to succeed	previous experience	tools and resources
fortunate accidents	self-confidence	trying new things
intelligence	supportive people	
making difficult choices	time	

PREPARE AND SPEAK

A. GATHER IDEAS Think about your discussion in the Consider the Ideas activity. Take brief notes on important ideas from your discussion about accidental discoveries. Include reasons that support your ideas.

B. ORGANIZE IDEAS Think of a personal discovery in your life. For example, think about a time when you discovered you had a talent for a sport or a subject in school. If you can't think of a personal discovery, borrow one from someone else's life experience.

1. How do the ideas in your notes from Activity A apply to this discovery?

2. Make notes about the major events involved in the discovery. List them in the order they happened. Say how this discovery affected you.

Personal discovery:

Events	Details

Effect:

C. SPEAK Use your notes to present your story. Remember to explain the steps in how the discovery occurred and how it affected you. As you tell your story, use one or more questions to maintain the interest of your listeners. Refer to the Self-Assessment checklist below before you begin.

iQ PRACTICE Go online for your alternate Unit Assignment.
Practice > Unit 7 > Activity 15

CHECK AND REFLECT

A. CHECK Think about the Unit Assignment as you complete the Self-Assessment checklist.

SELF-ASSESSMENT	Yes	No
I was able to speak easily about the topic.	☐	☐
My partner, group, and class understood me.	☐	☐
I used signal words.	☐	☐
I used vocabulary from the unit.	☐	☐
I used questions to maintain listeners' interest.	☐	☐
I linked words with vowels.	☐	☐

B. REFLECT Discuss these questions with a partner or group.

1. What is something new you learned in this unit?
2. Look back at the Unit Question—How can accidental discoveries affect our lives? Is your answer different now than when you started this unit? If yes, how is it different? Why?

iQ PRACTICE Go to the online discussion board to discuss the questions.
Practice > Unit 7 > Activity 16

TRACK YOUR SUCCESS

iQ PRACTICE Go online to check the words and phrases you have learned in this unit. *Practice > Unit 7 > Activity 17*

Check (✓) the skills and strategies you learned. If you need more work on a skill, refer to the page(s) in parentheses.

LISTENING	☐ I can listen for signal words and phrases. (p. 158)
NOTE-TAKING	☐ I can take notes on details. (p. 160)
VOCABULARY	☐ I can use collocations with prepositions. (p. 167)
GRAMMAR	☐ I can use indirect speech. (p. 169)
PRONUNCIATION	☐ I can link words with vowels. (p. 171)
SPEAKING	☐ I can use questions to maintain listener interest. (p. 172)
CRITICAL THINKING	☐ I can combine ideas from different sources. (p. 174)
OBJECTIVE ▶	☐ I can gather information and ideas to tell a personal story about an accidental discovery I made and how it affected me.

Engineering 8

LISTENING	listening for causes and effects
NOTE-TAKING	taking notes on causes and effects
CRITICAL THINKING	making appraisals
VOCABULARY	idioms
GRAMMAR	real conditionals
PRONUNCIATION	thought groups
SPEAKING	adding to another speaker's comments

UNIT QUESTION

What are the consequences of progress?

A. Discuss these questions with your classmates.

1. What are some important inventions of the past 50 years? How did they change people's lives for the better?

2. What are some unintended consequences of recent inventions? What problems that we face now are the result of "progress"?

3. Look at the photo. What technology is shown here? How could this technology be used?

B. Listen to *The Q Classroom* online. Then answer these questions.

1. Sophy and Marcus talk about some problems using smartphones can cause. Can you think of any others?

2. According to Felix, the pros of using smartphones might outweigh the cons. Do you agree? Why or why not?

iQ PRACTICE Go to the online discussion board to discuss the Unit Question with your classmates. *Practice > Unit 8 > Activity 1*

UNIT OBJECTIVE ▶ Listen to a radio interview and a lecture and gather information and ideas to present your opinions about the consequences of progress.

LISTENING

LISTENING 1 — Automation and Us

OBJECTIVE ▶ You are going to listen to a radio interview about automation from the Canadian Broadcasting Corporation. It explores some of the consequences of the use of machines to do work that was previously done by people. As you listen to the interview, gather information and ideas about the consequences of progress.

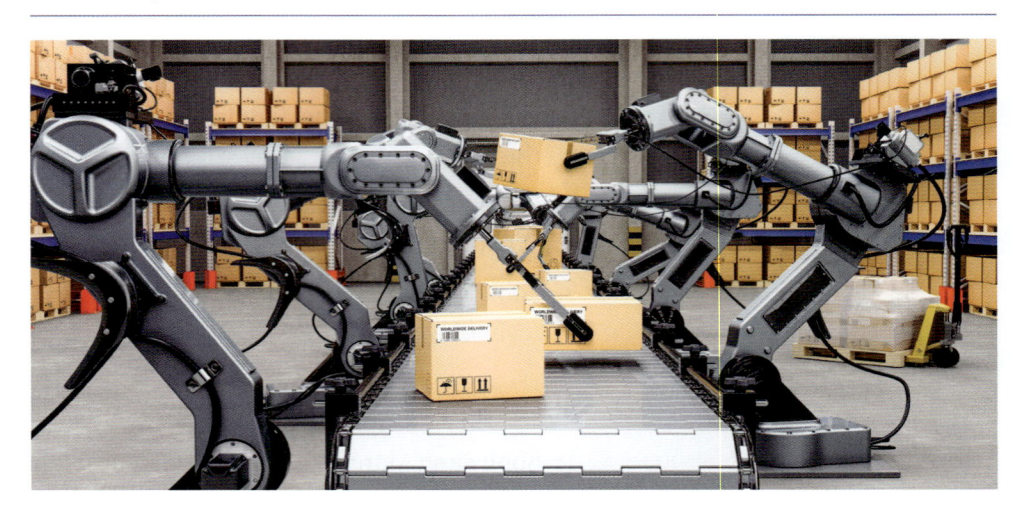

PREVIEW THE LISTENING

A. PREVIEW What do you think are some consequences of automation? Look at the photos of three different advancements. Make a note about a possible positive consequence and a possible negative consequence. Then discuss your answers with a partner.

+	+	+
−	−	−

UNIT 8   What are the consequences of progress?

B. VOCABULARY Read aloud these words from Listening 1. Check (✓) the ones you know. Use a dictionary to define any new or unknown words. Then discuss with a partner how the words will relate to the unit.

dependency *(n.)*	**generic** *(adj.)*	**necessarily** *(adv.)* OPAL
diversity *(n.)* OPAL	**idle** *(adj.)*	**philosophical** *(adj.)*
engagement *(n.)*	**intimate** *(adj.)*	**subtle** *(adj.)*
fulfilled *(adj.)*	**manual** *(adj.)*	**uniformity** *(n.)*

Oxford 5000™ words   OPAL Oxford Phrasal Academic Lexicon

iQ PRACTICE Go online to listen and practice your pronunciation.
Practice > Unit 8 > Activity 2

WORK WITH THE LISTENING

A. LISTEN AND TAKE NOTES Listen to the radio interview and use the chart below to take notes on the unexpected effects of automation.

iQ RESOURCES Go online to download extra vocabulary support.
Resources > Extra Vocabulary > Unit 8

Type of automation	Expected effects	Unexpected effects
medical record-keeping	- doctors would become more efficient	- -
automatic pilot systems	- flying would become safer	-

B. EXTEND Work with a partner. Use your notes to summarize the consequences of automation. Did any surprise you? Explain why.

C. IDENTIFY Match each cause with its effect.

____ 1. People are working.

____ 2. Doctors bring tablets into exam rooms.

____ 3. Much of our work involves data entry and looking at screens.

____ 4. Automated systems are used to fly airplanes.

____ 5. Pilots fall out of practice manually operating an airplane.

a. People are doing less diverse and creative work.

b. People are generally safer.

c. People get more unnecessary medical tests.

d. People are in danger when automatic systems fail.

e. People are happier and more fulfilled.

D. IDENTIFY Listen to the radio interview again. Circle the answer that best completes each statement.

1. According to Nicholas Carr, people tend to feel more satisfied if they are working because ____.
   a. they make money to support their families
   b. they can use their talents to overcome challenges
   c. they can use automation to make their jobs easier

2. People assumed that automation would allow doctors to ____.
   a. share information more easily
   b. see more patients in a day
   c. order more unnecessary tests

3. Tablets and computers are actually causing a lack of intimacy between doctors and patients because ____.
   a. doctors are assuming that patients need more tests than they actually do
   b. doctors are busier entering data into a computer, and they don't have time to talk to their patients
   c. doctors aren't making eye contact with their patients as much during a visit

4. According to Nicholas Carr, when we do more of our work using automation, our work becomes ____.
   a. more uniform and less interesting
   b. more diverse and skillful
   c. more satisfying

5. Because automation has taken over the physical job of a pilot, ____.

   a. pilots are free to concentrate on flying the plane more safely

   b. pilots manually fly the plane for about three minutes every flight

   c. pilots have totally forgotten how to respond in an emergency

E. **IDENTIFY** Read the statements. Check (✓) the opinions that Nicholas Carr would probably agree with. Then compare your answers with a partner and explain your choices.

   ☐ 1. "This concern about automation is a little exaggerated. Unless you work in a factory, you are not going to lose your job to a robot."

   ☐ 2. "Automation is the future, whether we like it or not. We need to learn how to develop automation that complements what humans are already good at."

   ☐ 3. "Increased automation in the workforce is most certainly going to result in an increased demand for creativity. Robots can do the boring work, and we'll do the fun, imaginative work."

   ☐ 4. "One of the dangers we need to think about as automation becomes the norm for many of us is that it may cause humans to become lazy. We might lose the ability to perform important skills."

   ☐ 5. "Government or industry leaders need to start thinking about a strategic way forward so that the decisions we make about automation aren't guided by what technology can do for us but by what it should do for us."

VOCABULARY SKILL REVIEW

Remember to use context to figure out the meaning of a word that is new to you. The sentence in which the word appears and even the text as a whole may contain clues about the word's meaning.

F. VOCABULARY Here are some words from Listening 1. Read the sentences. Then write the number of each bold word next to the correct definition.

1. As we grow up, our **dependency** on our parents decreases.
2. Rainforests are important because they are home to a great deal of plant and animal **diversity**.
3. I made my children leave their smartphones at home for a whole day with the family. When they bring them, I see less **engagement** between them.
4. I'm really **fulfilled** in my current job. I have no interest in applying for a different position.
5. As an artist, his goal is to produce unique, creative pieces. He does not want his art to feel **generic** and unoriginal.
6. I took three weeks of vacation over the summer. It felt wonderful to just be **idle** and not rushing around.
7. It's important that doctors develop an **intimate** relationship with their patients so they are comfortable discussing personal health matters.
8. I went to college so I could avoid doing **manual** labor.
9. The number of tickets is **necessarily** limited due to the size of the theater.
10. We were having a **philosophical** debate about good and evil.
11. He gave **subtle** hints about what gift he wanted for his birthday, but even though he wasn't direct, I could still guess.
12. In the suburbs, there is often a **uniformity** to the houses so that many in a neighborhood will look the same.

____ a. (*adj.*) shared by, including, or typical of a whole group of things; not specific

____ b. (*adj.*) involving using the hands or physical strength

____ c. (*adj.*) feeling happy and satisfied that you are doing something useful with your life

____ d. (*adv.*) used to say that something cannot be avoided

____ e. (*n.*) the fact of not varying and of being the same in all parts and at all times

____ f. (*n.*) a range of many people or things that are very different from each other

____ g. (*adj.*) not working hard

____ h. (*adj.*) connected with philosophy

____ i. (*n.*) the state of relying on somebody/something for something

____ j. (*adj.*) having a close and friendly relationship

____ k. (*n.*) being involved with somebody/something in an attempt to understand them/it

____ l. (*adj.*) not very noticeable or obvious

iQ PRACTICE Go online for more practice with the vocabulary.
Practice > Unit 8 > Activity 3

iQ PRACTICE Go online for additional listening and comprehension.
Practice > Unit 8 > Activity 4

SAY WHAT YOU THINK

DISCUSS Work in a group to discuss the questions.

1. Would you prefer to see a doctor who uses an automated system to store your medical records or one who uses paper files? Why?

2. What are some solutions to the problems described in Listening 1? Should governments set a policy limiting the development of automation? Should customers complain?

LISTENING SKILL Listening for causes and effects

A speaker may talk about what **causes** something to happen or what **happens because of** some other action or event. Speakers usually use **signal words** that connect two events or ideas.

These are some of the signal words that speakers use to show a **cause**.

because (of)   as a result of   due to   since   by

> **Due to** our belief that we don't like to work, we might think we want to be free from labor.
>
> **Because** doctors bring tablets into the exam room, they are less connected with their patients.
>
> **Since** we are trading deep engagement with the world for interaction with computers, we might be less satisfied with our work.

These are some of the signal words that speakers use to show a **result**.

because of this / that   as a result   therefore   so   the result is

> A lot of our time is spent looking at screens. **The result is** uniformity in activities, skills, and talent.
>
> Doctors now are not as connected with their patients, **so** they may miss important information they would have noticed before.
>
> Architects and lawyers are finding their work is increasingly involving data entry; **therefore**, they are engaging with the world differently than before.

Knowing these words and phrases will help you understand how the information is organized and predict what a speaker will say next.

ACADEMIC LANGUAGE

There are several other phrases we use to signal causes and effects in speech:
the effect(s) of
what happens if
what happens to
one of the reasons
the reason for
the reason why
so that
to see how

As you speak, try to use different phrases to introduce causes and effects so your speech is interesting and varied.

OPAL
Oxford Phrasal Academic Lexicon

iQ RESOURCES Go online to watch the Listening Skill Video.
Resources > Video > Unit 8 > Listening Skill Video

A. IDENTIFY Listen to the sentences. Circle the word or phrase you hear in each sentence.

Sentence 1
a. as a result of
b. the result is

Sentence 2
a. therefore
b. because of this

Sentence 3
a. because of
b. due to

Sentence 4
a. as a result
b. the result is

Sentence 5
a. therefore
b. because

Sentence 6
a. since
b. now that

B. CATEGORIZE Read each sentence. Is the underlined section the *cause* or the *effect*? Write *C* (cause) or *E* (effect).

TIP FOR SUCCESS

When listening to a presentation that mentions causes and effects, mark each cause or effect in your notes. Label them with a *C* or an *E*. This will help you make important connections when you review.

____ 1. Since <u>automation often allows companies to lower costs</u>, we can expect to see lower prices as well.

____ 2. Due to increased automation, <u>travel agents have experienced employment declines</u>.

____ 3. People are concerned about losing good jobs to automation, so <u>they argue that it should be limited to dirty or dangerous jobs</u>.

____ 4. Other people are worried that automation could cause worldwide unemployment. Therefore, <u>they are calling for universal basic income, where the government pays all adults whether they are working or not</u>.

____ 5. Despite these fears, we need to remember that economic growth could be negatively affected as a result of <u>limits placed on automation</u>.

____ 6. Since <u>it looks like automation developments are here to stay</u>, we need to do more to help workers transition from threatened jobs into new jobs.

iQ PRACTICE Go online for more practice listening for causes and effects.
Practice > Unit 8 > Activity 5

NOTE-TAKING SKILL Taking notes on causes and effects

When you are listening to a report, a lecture, an interview, or any kind of presentation that deals with causes and effects, list the causes and effects separately. One way to do this is by using a T-chart. Write causes on one side of the chart and effects on the other side. This will help you understand how the causes and effects relate to each other, and it will make reviewing your notes easier.

A. IDENTIFY Listen and read this section of a lecture on the benefits of digital cameras. Circle the words and phrases that introduce the causes. Underline the words and phrases that introduce effects.

Digital camera technology has made it possible for just about anyone anywhere to take pictures of anything. When you take a picture, the camera captures light rays that enter through the lens. Engineers invented an image sensor chip. When light hits the chip, it basically turns the light rays into a long number. Because of this, they have been able to put digital cameras into our smartphones. Since smartphones are available to almost everyone, it means that everyone can take pictures whenever they have their phones. Also, because digital images are essentially numbers, the pictures we take are easy to edit. We don't need to hire professional photographers as often because we can do the work ourselves for free. So, these days, regular people can take pictures of everything from their meals to events of political or historical importance. While this has resulted in some very silly pictures on the Internet, it has also meant that we can find out about current events more quickly because we are all "journalists" now. The consequences of this change are yet to be determined.

B. CATEGORIZE Complete the student's notes by writing down the missing causes and effects. Listen again if needed.

Causes	Effects
engineers invented _____	- cameras put into smartphones
smartphones are everywhere	- _____
digital pictures = _____	- _____
	- we don't hire photographers as often
people everywhere can take pictures	- _____ - _____

iQ PRACTICE Go online for more practice taking notes on causes and effects.
Practice > Unit 8 > Activity 6

LISTENING 2   Driverless Cars

OBJECTIVE ▶ You are going to listen to a lecture in an engineering class. As you listen, gather information and ideas about the consequences of progress.

PREVIEW THE LISTENING

A. PREVIEW This lecture is about driverless cars. How much do you know about them? How comfortable would you be riding in one? Discuss with a partner.

B. VOCABULARY Read aloud these words from Listening 2. Check (✓) the ones you know. Use a dictionary to define any new or unknown words. Then discuss with a partner how the words will relate to the unit.

abstract *(adj.)*	gut *(n.)*	outcome *(n.)* OPAL
cater to *(v. phr.)*	harm *(n.)* OPAL	prospective *(adj.)*
dive into *(v. phr.)*	loosely *(adv.)*	theoretically *(adv.)* OPAL
entirely *(adv.)* OPAL	notion *(n.)* OPAL	

Oxford 5000™ words   OPAL Oxford Phrasal Academic Lexicon

iQ PRACTICE Go online to listen and practice your pronunciation.
Practice > Unit 8 > Activity 7

WORK WITH THE LISTENING

A. LISTEN AND TAKE NOTES Listen to the lecture and complete the chart. Then compare your chart with a partner.

iQ RESOURCES Go online to download extra vocabulary support.
Resources > Extra Vocabulary > Unit 8

Causes	Effects
Workers not driving	
People not behind the wheel	
Cars can be programmed to do least harm in an accident	

LISTENING 2   189

B. IDENTIFY Read the sentences. Circle the answer that best completes each statement.

1. Some experts are predicting that, because of driverless cars, ____.
   a. millions of jobs will disappear
   b. more accidents will happen
   c. cars will still look the same

2. We may not need to buy insurance because driverless cars will ____.
   a. never crash
   b. be completely safe
   c. never make human errors

3. Our notion of what a car looks like will change ____.
   a. based on insurance companies' rules
   b. to provide us with things to do while on the road
   c. as a result of changes in the economy

4. When they are asked, most people say that cars should be programmed to ____.
   a. make decisions that do the least harm
   b. protect the weakest members of society
   c. make the same decisions that a human would make

5. When people were asked who a driverless car should protect if they were passengers, they said ____.
   a. the car should always protect the youngest, healthiest pedestrian
   b. they wanted the car to be programmed to do the least harm
   c. they wouldn't buy a car that didn't protect the passenger

6. Self-driving cars are an example of technological progress ____.
   a. with unintended consequences
   b. that causes many problems
   c. making life better for everyone

C. APPLY Listen again. Complete these sentences.

1. As a result of the invention of driverless cars, truck stops
   _____.

2. Because of driverless cars, car designers
   _____.

3. Due to the creation of movie cars and spa cars,
   _____.

4. People don't want to buy a car that wouldn't protect them, so
   _____.

5. Overall, driverless cars will reduce the number of accidents. Because of this,
   _____.

D. DISCUSS Work in a small group to discuss the questions.

1. Who should be responsible for helping people who lose their jobs as driverless cars become more common? Should the government help them find new employment? How?

2. If you were a designer of a driverless car, what special features would you include in your design to make traveling more comfortable and enjoyable for passengers?

3. How do you feel about cars having the power to make life-or-death decisions? What are some advantages and disadvantages of this?

4. Some people predict that car ownership will decline and people will order driverless cars to take them places rather than pay to buy and maintain a personal vehicle. Would you prefer to order or own a car?

E. **VOCABULARY** Here are some words from Listening 2. Complete each sentence with the correct word.

abstract *(adj.)*	cater to *(v. phr.)*	dive into *(v. phr.)*	entirely *(adv.)*
gut *(n.)*	harm *(n.)*	loosely *(adv.)*	notion *(n.)*
outcome *(n.)*	prospective *(adj.)*	theoretically *(adv.)*	

1. It's easy to understand the meaning of new English words when you can see a photo, but understanding _____ vocabulary can be more difficult.

2. When you work in a kitchen, you have to be careful not to _____ yourself with anything very hot or sharp.

3. When I take on a new project, I just _____ the work.

4. I'm not sure if it will work, but _____ the plans make sense.

5. Children's stores usually _____ a younger customer.

6. The movie is _____ based on the novel. The plot is similar, but there are some pretty big differences.

7. When he met her, he knew in his _____ that she was the right person for him to spend the rest of his life with.

8. The contest is really close, and people are very curious about the _____.

9. I really wasn't sure what the class was about. I only had the _____ that we would be learning about philosophy.

10. She spent the day showing the house to _____ buyers, but no one made an offer to buy it.

11. Their menu was almost _____ made up of pizza and pasta. There weren't many other options.

iQ PRACTICE Go online for more practice with the vocabulary.
Practice > Unit 8 > Activity 8

CRITICAL THINKING STRATEGY

Making appraisals

In Unit 5, you learned about evaluating information. Evaluating information allows you to make appraisals. When we read or listen to information, we may need to give a value to the information or the topic of the text based on the facts and opinions the text contains. When you come across new information, you need to think about where it is coming from and use your background knowledge to judge if the claims seem reasonable. Then you can use your evaluation of the information to decide how much of your money, time, or energy something is worth. This demonstrates a deeper understanding of the material and allows us to make informed decisions about information we receive.

iQ PRACTICE Go online to watch the Critical Thinking Video and check your comprehension. *Practice > Unit 8 > Activity 9*

F. IDENTIFY Look at the advertisements. Make an appraisal of the products they describe. For each product, decide whether you would be willing to pay the average price, a lower price, or a higher price. Discuss your answers with a partner.

"Nine out of ten dentists agree that Toothy Toothpaste is the most effective toothpaste on the market for preventing cavities."

"Engineers believe the Wave is the safest car available to consumers, and the Wave is the winner of three national safety awards."

"Researchers agree that the future of weight loss is the Weight Loss Winner pill. Just one pill a day melts the fat away."

G. DISCUSS Work with a partner. Answer the questions about each advertisement.

1. Where is the information coming from? Can you believe the "experts"? Why or why not?

2. Think about what you know about life and what you learned in school. Does the information in each advertisement seem possible? Why or why not?

WORK WITH THE VIDEO

A. PREVIEW In some places, driverless trucks are already being used. Look at the picture below. How would you feel if you were sitting in the passenger seat of a driverless semitrailer truck? What concerns would you have?

VIDEO VOCABULARY

disrupt *(v.)* to make it difficult for something to continue in the normal way

freight *(n.)* goods that are transported by ships, planes, trains, or trucks

pedal *(n.)* a part of a bicycle, car, etc., that you push or press with your foot to make the machine move or work

from scratch *(idm.)* from the very beginning, not using any of the work done before

traitor *(n.)* a person who works against their friends, country, etc.

remotely *(adv.)* from a distance

autonomously *(adv.)* with the ability to work without any help from anyone

iQ RESOURCES Go online to watch the video about new technology that may soon make many trucks driverless. *Resources > Video > Unit 8 > Unit Video*

B. IDENTIFY Watch the video two or three times. Take notes about the effects that driverless technology could have on the world.

Causes	Effects
Stefan and his team are adapting existing trucks.	
Stefan and his team added a computer to control a truck's pedals and steering wheel.	
Stefan's type of self-driving truck will still require drivers.	
Stefan and his team are focusing specifically on highway driving.	

C. **DISCUSS** Read the quotation from the speaker in this video and answer the questions. Discuss with a partner.

"Once you're out there doing it and you're dealing with real-life problems, things going slightly wrong, fixing them up, you can then demonstrate to the world that we have made this thing work. We're not going to wait around for all the regulations. And then almost by virtue of demonstrating its power, it forces the world to change around it."

1. Do you think this is a good way to cause change?
2. What are some of the potential consequences of changes that come too quickly?

SAY WHAT YOU THINK

SYNTHESIZE Think about Listening 1, Listening 2, and the unit video as you discuss the questions.

1. In general, does making progress usually have positive or negative consequences? What examples can you think of to support your opinion?
2. Whose job should it be to regulate progress? An international agency, like the United Nations? The government in each country? Businesses? Scientists and engineers?

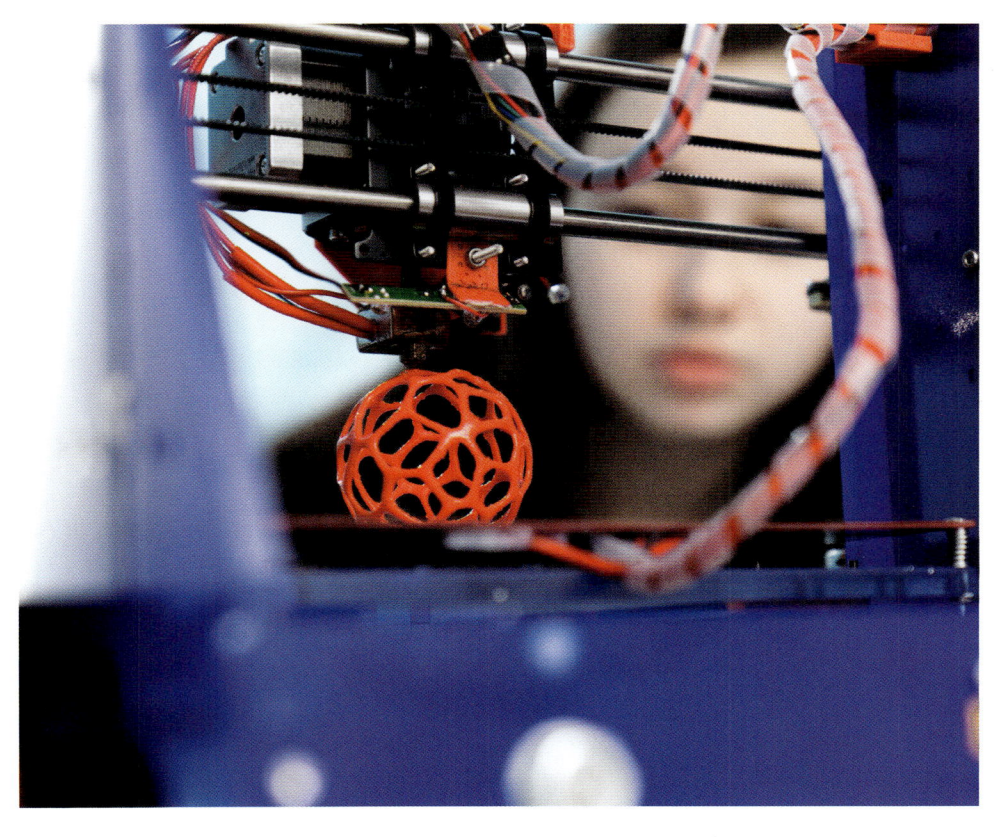

VOCABULARY SKILL   Idioms

An **idiom** is a particular group of words that has a specific meaning different from the individual words in it. Idioms function as a separate unit, almost as if they were a single word.

On the other hand means "in contrast."

⌐ But **on the other hand**, isn't flying, for instance, safer than ever before, thanks to
∟ automation?

Fall victim to means "to be negatively affected by something."

⌐ Pilots often **fall victim to** what researchers call "automation complacency."

Because idioms have specific meanings, much like individual words do, it is useful to remember these "chunks" of language in the same way you memorize individual words.

There are thousands of idioms. Most of these idioms are not in the dictionary. For this reason, it is important that you notice them when they occur and use context clues to figure out their meaning.

A. IDENTIFY Listen to the excerpts from Listening 1 and Listening 2. Listen for each idiom and how it is used. Then match each idiom with its definition in the box.

a. something to worry about
b. remember
c. not as good as it used to be because you have not been practicing
d. at risk
e. with no particular activities; free

____ 1. at leisure

____ 2. rusty

____ 3. cause for concern

____ 4. on the line

____ 5. keep in mind

TIP FOR SUCCESS
Idioms can be difficult to understand, especially in conversation. When someone uses an idiom you are not familiar with, use a clarification strategy. You can also use context to understand the meaning, and some idioms can be found in a collocations dictionary.

B. COMPOSE Create sentences using the five idioms in Activity A. Practice saying the sentences with a partner.

iQ PRACTICE   Go online for more practice using idioms.
Practice > Unit 8 > Activity 10

SPEAKING

OBJECTIVE ▶ At the end of this unit, you are going share your opinions about the consequences of progress. As you speak, you will need to add to other speakers' comments.

GRAMMAR Real conditionals

Real conditional sentences show a possible or expected cause and effect. They can give information about the present or the future.

Most real conditionals have a conditional clause containing *if* and a simple present verb connected to a main clause with a simple present or future verb.

    [conditional clause] [main clause]
    If driverless cars **become** popular, people **will** lose their jobs.
    (People will lose their jobs as a result of driverless cars becoming popular.)

Conditional clauses can also begin with *when* or *whenever* to describe a general truth or habit.

    [conditional clause] [main clause]
    When a doctor **has** a computer, the doctor **will order** more diagnostic tests.
    (Doctors order more tests as a result of having a computer.)

The conditional clause can come before or after the main clause. If the conditional clause comes first, there is a pause, shown by a comma, between the clauses.

    If you don't have to drive, how do you spend your time?
    How do you spend your time if you don't have to drive?

Real conditionals can be used to express many kinds of ideas.

Things that will become true
- [ ] If he can find old wood, Rick will make a guitar.

Predictions
- [ ] If we don't have to drive cars anymore, how they look will change.

Habits
- [ ] When doctors bring their computers into an exam room, they order more tests.

Deals, compromises, and promises
- [ ] "I'll make Bob Dylan a guitar from Chumley's wood if he asks."

Advice
- [ ] If you rely too much on automation, do a couple of things manually each day.

Warnings
- [ ] When pilots don't get enough manual practice, they make mistakes in emergency situations.

Instructions
- [ ] When you see someone throwing away old wood, grab it from them.

A. APPLY Read the sentences. Rewrite or restate each one so that the conditional clause comes first. Then practice saying the sentences with a partner.

1. More automation is not necessarily good when it isn't designed to benefit humans.

2. We can require pilots to practice flying manually if we are worried about their skills getting rusty.

3. You should think about getting into a different industry if you are worried about a robot replacing you.

4. I don't like getting more medical tests when I don't need them.

5. I'll buy an exercise car when they are invented.

6. They'll redesign cars when they all become driverless.

7. You can't be sure of people's answers if you don't ask them the question.

8. Automation advancements are certain if things continue as we expect.

B. COMPOSE For each situation, write a conditional sentence using the type of conditional in parentheses. Then compare answers with a partner.

1. A car company wants to sell a driverless car that is programmed to protect pedestrians in case of an emergency. (warning)

2. Your friend just bought a driverless car. You'd like a ride. In exchange, you can offer to pay for the gas. (deal)

3. You believe that computers in cars will be able to communicate with each other in the next couple of years. (prediction)

4. Your friend is a journalist. She is worried about her job being taken by a computer programmed to write news stories. (advice)

iQ PRACTICE Go online for more practice with real conditionals.
Practice > Unit 8 > Activity 11

iQ PRACTICE Go online for the Grammar Expansion: review of real and unreal conditionals. *Practice > Unit 8 > Activity 12*

PRONUNCIATION Thought groups

Speakers don't talk in a steady, continuous stream of words. Instead, they say their words as **thought groups** to help listeners understand their ideas. Speakers separate thought groups with brief pauses.

A thought group may be a short sentence.

    Automation isn't always a good thing.
                thought group

It may be part of a longer sentence.

    I'm not worried | that robots will take over the planet.
    thought group 1   thought group 2

However, I think my father is suspicious | about his new virtual assistant.
thought group 1   thought group 2   thought group 3

It may be a word, a short phrase, or a clause. The end of a sentence is always the end of the thought group.

    Ultimately, | we usually like technology | that makes life easier.
    thought group 1   thought group 2   thought group 3

When speaking, think about how to form your ideas into thought groups to help your listeners understand your ideas.

A. IDENTIFY Listen to the speaker. Draw slashes (/) between the thought groups.

people always ask me what advice do you have for workers who are facing an increasingly automated workplace first get a college education experts agree that blue-collar jobs will be most in danger second focus on working in a job that machines and robots haven't proven very good at such as working with customers being creative planning managing people or directing finally if it looks like the writing is on the wall for your particular field of expertise be flexible consider transitioning to other work

B. APPLY Practice reading the sentences in Activity A with a partner. Focus on separating thought groups.

iQ PRACTICE Go online for more practice with thought groups.
Practice > Unit 8 > Activity 13

SPEAKING SKILL Adding to another speaker's comments

One way to keep a conversation interesting is **to build on someone else's ideas**. Sometimes you want to communicate that you agree with another speaker or add other ideas related to the topic.

These phrases can be used to add to the conversation.

To show agreement	To build on an idea
I agree	Plus . . .
That's a good point	Furthermore . . .
That's true	I would add that . . .
Right	Another important point is (that) . . .
Exactly	To build on what you said . . .
	Going back to what you before . . .

Phrases of agreement can be combined with phrases that build on an idea.

I agree. I would also add (that) . . .
Exactly. I would also add (that) . . .

Listen to the conversation.

Sung-ju: So, while I really enjoy using social media to keep in touch with friends and family, it's a bit creepy when the site automatically labels or tags my photos. I am all for intelligent machines, but I'm not sure I like the idea of my computer watching and remembering what I do.

David: <u>That's true! Plus,</u> I hate when social networking sites push advertisements that they think I'm interested in.

A. IDENTIFY Listen to a discussion about potential consequences of a common form of automation. Check (✓) the phrases of agreement and the building phrases you hear. Then work with a partner to summarize the main points.

☐ Another important point is that . . .   ☐ That's a good point.

☐ And to build on what John said earlier . . .   ☐ Exactly!

☐ Going back to what John said, . . .   ☐ I would add that . . .

B. EXTEND Create a list of at least four consequences of using voice recognition.

C. DISCUSS Work in a group. Discuss the reasons you listed in Activity B. Agree with or add to the ideas you hear.

iQ PRACTICE Go online for more practice adding to another speaker's comments. *Practice > Unit 8 > Activity 14*

UNIT ASSIGNMENT Share opinions about the consequences of progress

OBJECTIVE ▶

In this assignment, you are going share your opinions about the consequences of progress—both good and bad. As you prepare to share your opinions, think about the Unit Question, "What are the consequences of progress?" Use information from Listening 1, Listening 2, the unit video, and your work in this unit to support your opinions. Refer to the Self-Assessment checklist on page 202.

CONSIDER THE IDEAS

DISCUSS Work with a partner. Discuss the questions about technology and growing older.

1. What challenges do people face as they grow older?
2. What technological advancements have made life easier for elderly people?
3. What challenges do some older people have with technology? How will future products need to be adapted to be useful to older users?
4. Are there any possible negative consequences associated with older people using technology to improve their lifestyles?

PREPARE AND SPEAK

TIP FOR SUCCESS

When participating in a group discussion, write down ideas that you think of while others are speaking. This will help you to remember your ideas when you have an opportunity to take a turn.

A. GATHER IDEAS Look at the photos of technological advancements designed to improve the lives of elderly people. List two potential positive consequences and two potential negative consequences.

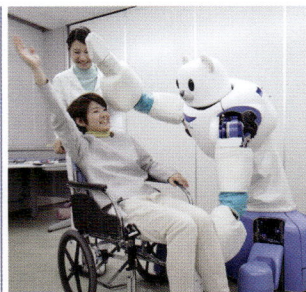

Robotic pet	Personal assistant	Medical caregiver
+	+	+
+	+	+
-	-	-
-	-	-

B. ORGANIZE IDEAS Work with a partner. Compare the positive and negative consequences you listed for each product in Activity A. Add to the chart.

C. **SPEAK** Work in a small group. Follow these steps. Refer to the Self-Assessment checklist below before you begin.

1. Conduct a group discussion on this topic: What are the consequences of elderly people using technology designed to improve their lives?

2. Take turns expressing your ideas. Try to use conditional sentences to express your ideas. Also try to use some of the phrases you learned to add to other speakers' comments. As you speak, use pauses to separate your thought groups.

3. As a group, try to reach a consensus about the most useful (and least potentially harmful) product. Which do you think you would most appreciate when you get older?

iQ PRACTICE Go online for your alternate Unit Assignment.
Practice > Unit 8 > Activity 15

CHECK AND REFLECT

CHECK Think about the Unit Assignment as you complete the Self-Assessment checklist.

SELF-ASSESSMENT	Yes	No
I was able to speak easily about the topic.	☐	☐
I took notes on causes and effects.	☐	☐
My partner, group, and class understood me.	☐	☐
I made appraisals.	☐	☐
I used real conditional sentences.	☐	☐
I used vocabulary from the unit.	☐	☐
I added to other speakers' comments.	☐	☐
I used thought groups while speaking.	☐	☐

D. **REFLECT** Discuss these questions with a partner or group.

1. What is something new you learned in this unit?

2. Look back at the Unit Question—What are the consequences of progress? Is your answer different now than when you started the unit? If yes, how is it different? Why?

iQ PRACTICE Go to the online discussion board to discuss the questions.
Practice > Unit 8 > Activity 16

TRACK YOUR SUCCESS

iQ PRACTICE Go online to check the words and phrases you have learned in this unit. *Practice > Unit 8 > Activity 17*

Check (✓) the skills and strategies you learned. If you need more work on a skill, refer to the page(s) in parentheses.

LISTENING	☐ I can listen for causes and effects. (p. 185)
NOTE-TAKING	☐ I can take notes on causes and effects. (p. 187)
CRITICAL THINKING	☐ I can make appraisals. (p. 193)
VOCABULARY	☐ I can understand idioms. (p. 196)
GRAMMAR	☐ I can use real conditional sentences. (p. 197)
PRONUNCIATION	☐ I can recognize and use thought groups. (p. 199)
SPEAKING	☐ I can add to another speaker's comments. (p. 200)
OBJECTIVE ▶	☐ I can gather information and ideas to share my opinions about the consequences of progress.

VOCABULARY LIST AND CEFR CORRELATION

The **Oxford 5000™** is an expanded core word list for advanced learners of English. The words have been chosen based on their frequency in the Oxford English Corpus and relevance to learners of English. As well as the **Oxford 3000™** core word list, the Oxford 5000 includes an additional 2,000 words that are aligned to the CEFR, guiding advanced learners at B2–C1 level on the most useful high-level words to learn to expand their vocabulary.

OPAL The **Oxford Phrasal Academic Lexicon** is an essential guide to the most important words and phrases to know for academic English. The word lists are based on the Oxford Corpus of Academic English and the British Academic Spoken English corpus.

The **Common European Framework of Reference for Language (CEFR)** provides a basic description of what language learners have to do to use language effectively. The system contains 6 reference levels: A1, A2, B1, B2, C1, C2.

UNIT 1

advance *(v.)* B2
assess *(v.)* OPAL B2
capable *(adj.)* OPAL B2
clarity *(n.)* C1
contact *(n.)* OPAL B1
effective *(adj.)* OPAL B1
enthusiasm *(n.)* B2
ethical *(adj.)* OPAL B2
executive *(n.)* B2
initiative *(n.)* OPAL B2
innovation *(n.)* B2
motivation *(n.)* OPAL B2
perspective *(n.)* OPAL B2
promote *(v.)* OPAL B1
realistic *(adj.)* B2
responsibility *(n.)* OPAL B1
role *(n.)* OPAL A2
style *(n.)* OPAL A1
take on *(v. phr.)* B1
title *(n.)* OPAL A1
versus *(prep.)* OPAL C1

UNIT 2

bias *(n.)* OPAL B2
chaos *(n.)* C1
embrace *(v.)* B2
feature *(n.)* OPAL A2
grant *(v.)* B2
imply *(v.)* OPAL B2
inflexible *(adj.)* C1
legal *(adj.)* OPAL B1
manufacture *(v.)* B2
moderately *(adv.)* C1
monopoly *(n.)* C1
obtain *(v.)* OPAL B2
open-minded *(adj.)* C1
point out *(v. phr.)* B1
purchase *(n.)* B2
recognize *(v.)* OPAL A2
revert *(v.)* C2
shade *(n.)* B2
stifle *(v.)* C1
stimulating *(adj.)* B2
stumble upon *(v. phr.)* C2
theme *(n.)* OPAL B1
trademark *(v.)* C1
turn out *(v. phr.)* B1

UNIT 3

agency *(n.)* B2
asset *(n.)* B2
balance *(v.)* OPAL B1
current *(adj.)* OPAL B1
debt *(n.)* B2
entrepreneur *(n.)* B2
insurance *(n.)* B2
interest *(n.)* OPAL A1
minor *(adj.)* OPAL B2
mortgage *(n.)* B2
naturally *(adv.)* OPAL B1
nutrition *(n.)* B2
pension *(n.)* B2
precisely *(adv.)* OPAL B2
retirement *(n.)* B2
series *(n.)* OPAL A2
set up *(v. phr.)* B1
spare *(n.)* C1
stock *(n.)* OPAL B2
tool *(n.)* OPAL A2
tedious *(adj.)* C1
truly *(adv.)* B2
weigh in *(v. phr.)* C2

UNIT 4

affordable *(adj.)* B2
alternative *(n.)* OPAL A2
astonishing *(adj.)* B2
capacity *(n.)* OPAL B2
double *(v.)* A2
dramatically *(adv.)* B2
extent *(n.)* OPAL B2
force *(n.)* OPAL B1
function *(v.)* OPAL B2
gear *(n.)* C1
hazardous *(adj.)* C1
hilarious *(adj.)* B2
intention *(n.)* OPAL B1
inventor *(n.)* B1
noticeable *(adj.)* C1

204

power *(v.)* B2
rapidly *(adv.)* OPAL B2
reflect *(v.)* OPAL B1
sophisticated *(adj.)* B2
stream *(v.)* C1
summarize *(v.)* OPAL B1
target *(n.)* OPAL A2
throughout *(prep.)* OPAL B1

UNIT 5

alter *(v.)* OPAL B2
buzz *(v.)* C1
compound *(v.)* C1
consumer *(n.)* B1
debate *(n.)* OPAL B2
distribute *(v.)* OPAL B2
disturbing *(adj.)* C1
dominate *(v.)* OPAL B2
ethics *(n.)* OPAL B2
ignorance *(n.)* C1
infection *(n.)* B2
intense *(adj.)* B2
load *(n.)* B2
modification *(n.)* C1
precision *(n.)* OPAL C1
productivity *(n.)* C1
reaction *(n.)* OPAL B1
revolution *(n.)* B2
suffer *(v.)* B1
survey *(n.)* OPAL A2
ultimate *(adj.)* OPAL B2

UNIT 6

altogether *(adv.)* B2
basically *(adv.)* OPAL B2
burst *(v.)* C1
confidence *(n.)* B2
decent *(adj.)* B2
disposable *(adj.)* C1
expand *(v.)* OPAL B1
fairness *(n.)* C1

fierce *(adj.)* C1
genius *(n.)* B2
in particular *(idm.)* OPAL B1
investor *(n.)* B2
launch *(v.)* B2
massive *(adj.)* B2
meaningful *(adj.)* OPAL C1
miserable *(adj.)* B2
predecessor *(n.)* C1
pressure *(n.)* OPAL B1
profit *(n.)* B1
rate *(n.)* OPAL A2
steadily *(adv.)* B2
values *(n.)* OPAL B1
vision *(n.)* B2
workforce *(n.)* B2

UNIT 7

ache *(v.)* A2
adhesive *(n.)* C2
adopt *(v.)* OPAL B2
alert *(adj.)* C1
biological *(adj.)* B2
deprived *(adj.)* C1
exploit *(v.)* OPAL B2
face to face *(adv. phr.)* C1
flammable *(adj.)* C2
inadvertent *(adj.)* C2
in all probability *(adv. phr.)* C1
inconceivable *(adj.)* C2
interact *(v.)* OPAL B2
mandatory *(adj.)* C1
obvious *(adj.)* OPAL B1
odds *(n.)* C1
reunion *(n.)* C1
synthetic *(adj.)* C1
unreliable *(adj.)* B1
vastly *(adv.)* B2

UNIT 8

abstract *(adj.)* B2
cater to *(v. phr.)* C1
dependency *(n.)* C1
dive into *(v. phr.)* C2
diversity *(n.)* OPAL B2
engagement *(n.)* C1
entirely *(adv.)* OPAL B2
fulfilled *(adj.)* B2
generic *(adj.)* C1
gut *(n.)* C1
harm *(n.)* OPAL B2
idle *(adj.)* C1
intimate *(adj.)* C1
loosely *(adv.)* C1
manual *(adj.)* C1
necessarily *(adv.)* OPAL B1
notion *(n.)* OPAL B2
outcome *(n.)* OPAL B2
philosophical *(adj.)* C1
prospective *(adj.)* C1
subtle *(adj.)* C1
theoretically *(adv.)* OPAL C1
uniformity *(n.)* C2